ILLUSTRATIONS ACKNOWLEDGEMENTS

Cover: Brigadier Hilary Cree; Marc Fallander (inset)

Illustrations supplied courtesy of: Agence France Presse 135 (middle and bottom), 137 (top left and bottom); Airphoto International 24, 58-59, 132 (bottom), 133 (bottom); Alain Evrard 138-139; Alan Birch 26, 38, 39 (top), 40, 48, 52 (middle), 53 (top right), 54 (bottom), 57, 64, 65, 66 (top), 68 (bottom), 72, 74 (bottom), 76 (right), 78 (top left, middle, bottom right), 79 (top and bottom left), 80, 100 (bottom), 123, 126 (bottom); Basic Law Consultative Committee 129 (bottom); Brigadier Hilary Cree 22 (right); British Parliamentary Papers, China 46; Building and Lands Department, Hong Kong Government 106, 111 (top); Chan Chik 96 (top), 107 (bottom left), 108, 110-111; Chinese University of Hong Kong 34; City Hall Library 68 (middle); Civil Aviation Department 89; David Chappell 142; David Mahoney 32 (left), 62 (bottom and middle); Dr B Mellor 104, 107 (top left and right), 132 (top); Frank A Crampton Collection, Professor Dilip K Basu, University of California 35; G C Hamilton 30 (top); Government Information Service, Hong Kong 33, 45 (top and bottom), 47 (top), 49 (bottom), 52 (bottom), 53 (top left), 76 (top left), 88, 90, 95, 96 (bottom), 98, 102, 105, 107 (bottom right), 109, 110 (top right), 112 (top), 118 (top), 120 (top), 122 (right), 125 (top), 127 (bottom), 131, 134 (bottom), 136 (bottom right), 138 (top left), 144, 148-149; Graphics Publications 27; Heirlooms 54 (top), 100 (top); H Chamberlain 114; Hongkong and Shanghai Banking Corporation 49 (top left and right), 79 (top and bottom right); Hong Kong Arts Centre 94; Hong Kong History Workshop, University of Hong Kong 76 (bottom left); Hong Kong Museum of Art 31 (left), 42-43, 45 (middle); Hong Kong Museum of History 23, 25, 63 (left), 122 (left); Hong Kong Public Records Office 32 (top), 51, 52 (top), 53 (middle, left and right, bottom right); Hong Kong Regiment Museum 62 (top), 67; Hongkong Standard 126 (top), 129 (top), 130, 135 (top), 137 (top right), 138 (bottom left), 145; Hong Kong University Press: end papers (front); Hulton Picture Collection 103 (top right); Immigration Department, Hong Kong Government 128; Imperial War Museum, London 70, 73 (second from bottom), 82 (bottom left and right), 83 (bottom), 84, 85, 86; Jacky Yip, China Photo Library: end papers (back); Jardine, Matheson and Company Ltd. 30 (bottom), 31 (right), 47 (bottom); John Stericker 71; Joint Services Public Relations Staff, British Forces 22 (left), 97, 113, 125 (bottom); Lady May Ride 81, 82 (top), 83 (top); Macleay Museum, University of Sydney 66 (bottom); Marc Fallander 127 (top); Ms Kao, Museum of Chinese Art, Chinese University of Hong Kong 63 (right); Narcotics Museum, Royal Hong Kong Police 44; New China News Agency 136 (top, middle and bottom left), 143 (bottom); Nigel Hicks 91, 150, 151; O J L Barnham 74 (top), 75; Public Archives Canada 78 (top right); Public Relations, Peninsula Group, Hong Kong 36, 37; Public Records Office, London 143; South China Morning Post 78 (bottom left), 99, 118 (bottom), 119, 120 (bottom), 124, 133 (top left and right), 134 (top), 136 (top right); Swire Archives 53 (bottom left), 56; Swire School of Design, Hong Kong Polytechnic 101; Topham 103 (top left and bottom), 111 (bottom), 112 (bottom, left and right); University of Hong Kong Library 68 (top), 69, 77, 121, 140; Wattis Fine Art 50; Yates Collection 39 (bottom), 73 (all apart from second from bottom)

Hong Kong
The Colony That Never Was

DEDICATION

For Sandra, Suk-yee, my wife and helpmate over my many years in Hong Kong. She is a Hong Kong person and an individual with precious rights. But, as this book is my monument to the Hong Kong of which she is an integral part, I feel very strongly that my dedication should be extended to all the Hong Kong people. They have achieved much: they deserve more—their own future.

Editor: Don J Cohn
Series Editor: Rose Borton
Illustrations Editor: Caroline Robertson
Design: Aubrey Tse
Cover Design: Kate Poole
Map Design: Winnie Sung

Production House: Twin Age Limited, Hong Kong
Printed in Hong Kong by Sing Cheong Printing Co., Ltd

End paper (front): Map of the San-On-District, drawn by Father Volontieri, May 1866
End paper (back): View of Central at dusk

Hong Kong
The Colony That Never Was

Alan Birch

HONG KONG: A QUESTION OF STATUS

'When Sir John Brembridge came to see me about the [Chinese] banks he was in a rage.'

'I've told them', he spluttered, 'they've got to toe the line, otherwise . . . otherwise, we'll *nationalise* them!'

'Oh, no, Sir John', I said, 'you *can't* say 'nationalise'—we're not a nation.'

'Well, we're a colony, aren't we?' he said, 'So we'll *colonise* them!'

'Oh *no*, Sir John', I explained, 'you *can't* say that, we *never* refer to Hong Kong as a "colony" these days.'

'Well then, what *are* we called then?'

'Well', I explained, 'these days we call ourselves a "territory".'

'Right, then!', said Sir John, 'we'll *terrorise* them!'

Anecdote recounted by Sir Philip Haddon Cave (KBE, CMG, JP)
in a farewell address to the Foreign Correspondents' Club,
Hong Kong, 30 May, 1985.

Hong Kong

AUTHOR'S PREFACE

I have long wanted to write a book like this, which would be my own monument not only to Hong Kong's remarkable achievements and history, but also as a kind of memento of my many pleasant years spent here in Hong Kong, first as a teacher of history at Hong Kong University; then in the post-1984 period in retirement. In the course of these long and eventful years here, I have made many old and trusted friends who have given me constant support for this work. I would like to mention Ms Charlotte Havilland, Archivist of the Swire Group in London and in particular, my old university friend, Dr Bernard Mellor, whose unfailing kindness, and unfeigned interest in Hong Kong history never failed to inspire me.

Back in 1984, when it seemed as if the project had come up to the boil with the completion of negotiations and the signing of the Sino-British Joint Declaration, my own map of Hong Kong's past and future, up to 1997, was complete. All I had to do was to sort out my ideas and my pictures and the book would emerge as a memorial to the British presence in my adopted city-state.

The realization of this book is due solely to the patience and persistence of my publishers at Odyssey—in particular Mr Magnus Bartlett, who supplied the aerial photographs of Hong Kong, which sum up the physical state of Hong Kong today and Mr Geoffrey Cloke, for his quiet and reassuring business-like approach to my project. I would also like to thank Matthew Turner of the Hong Kong Polytechnic who supplied me with many interesting details on Hong Kong's industrialisation and Sarah Lock for her patience in photographing the exhibits. Finally, it is a pleasure to thank my friend Ms Jan Morris for lending her authority as an imperial historian in this book by writing a most perceptive foreword to my history.

Alan Birch,
Hong Kong, March 1991

CONTENTS

FOREWORD

This book is subtly titled, because it tells the tale of a great historical ambiguity. *The Colony That Never Was* can be read as shorthand for all the political anomalies, constitutional complexities and geographical surprises that make the story of Hong Kong unique. Although the territory was officially British throughout the years recorded in this book, it was hardly a colony in the normal British sense, being very unlike the rest of the 50-odd Crown Colonies which, in the heyday of the British Empire, speckled the map of the world with red. It was governed like many others, but it was different in kind.

After 1898, much of Hong Kong was held only on a 99-year lease from another power, meaning that even in the prime of imperial ideology it could hardly be considered an absolute imperial possession. Nor was it ever exactly colonized—its population was always overwhelmingly un-British, and the British people who went to administer it or profit from it seldom intended to stay for long. It was in fact no more than a British foothold on somebody else's territory, somebody else's civilization: Hong Kong was essentially an integral part of China, and there was never a chance of its achieving, like most other British dependencies, its own national independence.

More ambiguous still is the proof of Hong Kong's status in the post-imperial world of the late twentieth century. The British Empire has almost disappeared, and Hong Kong itself has become a less orthodox possession than ever. It still flies the British flag, is still presided over by a British governor, but is essentially a Chinese metropolis with international overtones. The political destiny of this city-state may still be in the hands of London, but economically it has long since become a power in its own right, a great manufacturing centre, and one of the world's key financial exchanges.

And the greatest ambiguity of all concerns the end of this un-colony. Due to be handed over to Chinese sovereignty at the expiry of its lease, and thus no longer to be a separate entity at all, it is spending the last decade of its life contemplating the exact day—1 July 1997—when it will cease to exist. What other place on earth can contemplate a finite future? Mr Birch's book comes just in time, for within our lifetimes it may well be that British Hong Kong will all but be forgotten, swept from the everyday consciousness, leaving behind it a few old buildings, a few regrets and perhaps a few liberties—almost as though, indeed, it had never been.

Jan Morris

CHRONOLOGY OF HONG KONG 1841-1997

1841		Hong Kong ceded to Britain by China.
	January	Captain Charles Elliot becomes Chief Superintendent of Trade.
		Jardine, Matheson and Company erect house and godowns at East Point.
		First land sales.
1842		Hong Kong proclaimed a free port.
	February	Establishment of Superintendent of Trade moved from Macau to Hong Kong.
	August	Treaty of Nanking confirms cession of Hong Kong to Britain (ratified in June 1843).
1843		Arrival of Keying, Chinese Imperial Commissioner in Hong Kong.
		Queen's Road laid out.
		Public announcement of Royal Charter 'erecting Hong Kong as a separate colony'.
	June	Sir Henry Pottinger becomes Hong Kong's first governor.
1844		Sir John Davis proclaimed governor.
		Attempt to regulate population (20,000) by Registration Ordinance opposed by general strikes.
1845		*China Mail* newspaper published.
	February	US Consul appointed.
	August	Peninsular and Oriental Steam Navigation Company commences monthly mail route calling at Hong Kong.
1846	*May*	Hong Kong Club opens in Queen's Road Central.
1848	*March*	Departure of Governor Sir John Davis.
		Governor Sir Samuel Bonham takes over.
1849		Completion of St John's Anglican Cathedral.
1851	*June*	Cricket Club established.
1852		Taiping Rebellion refugees arrive in Hong Kong.
		Beginning of construction of Government House.
1854		Governor Sir John Bowring in office.
1855	*February*	Last public executions in Hong Kong.
1856	*June*	Development at Pokfulam for villages and farms to grow ginger and coffee.
1857	*January*	British Consul declares war on China (Arrow War).
		Five-hundred Europeans poisoned by arsenic in bread made at E Sing Bakery.
	June	Establishment of Aberdeen Docks by Douglas Lapraik and Captain Lam.
	October	Inaugural issue of *Hong Kong Daily Press*.
1858	*June*	Treaty of Tientsin signed, legalising opium sales in China.
1859	*March*	Sir John Bowring recommends annexation of Kowloon for commercial and health reasons.
	September	Sir Hercules Robinson becomes governor.
1860	*August*	Kowloon Peninsula chosen as camp for Allied Expeditionary Forces to China.
		Enquiry into civil service abuses.

	October	Convention of Peking ratified formalising lease of Kowloon Peninsula and Stonecutters Island to Britain in perpetuity.
1861	March	Hong Kong General Chamber of Commerce founded.
1861-71		Botanical Gardens laid out.
1862	December	Battle of Tsim Sha Tsui between local Punti and Hakka tribes.
1863		Jardine, Matheson establishes telegraph line from Central to Causeway Bay. Hong Kong issues silver dollar coins.
1864	November	Gas street lighting introduced.
1865		Hongkong and Shanghai Banking Corporation founded.
1866	April	Hong Kong Royal Mint opens. Sir Richard Macdonnell becomes governor.
1867		The blockade of Hong Kong—Chinese customs cruisers patrol Hong Kong waters, levying duties on junks trading with non-treaty ports.
	August	Praya walls destroyed by typhoon: several large vessels and junks lost.
1868		Mint closed due to operating losses. Tung Wah Hospital opened by Governor Sir Richard Macdonnell.
1869	November	Visit of HRH Duke of Edinburgh and Royal Opening of City Hall.
1870		Hong Kong—Amoy—Shanghai cable opens for traffic. Completion of submarine telegraphic cable link to China.
1871	June	Hong Kong—Singapore cable begins operation.
1872		Sir Arthur Kennedy becomes governor.
1873		First newspaper under sole Chinese management published.
1874	September	Major typhoon—35 foreign ships sunk, over 2,000 people dead, about HK$5 million of property lost or destroyed.
1875		Committee formed in Hong Kong to raise subscriptions for endowment of professorship in Chinese at Oxford University. James Legge, local missionary, appointed to the post.
1877	April	Sir John Pope Hennessy proclaimed governor.
	May	Ng Choy, first Chinese barrister, admitted to the bar. First Chinese civil marriage in Hong Kong.
	November	Budget exceeds HK$1 million. First steam laundry established.
1878	May	Iron works at Shau Kei Wan established.
1879		Secular system of education introduced to government schools. Grant-in-aid schools to have freedom of religious instruction.

1880	April	First rickshaws used.
	May	Telegraphic link with the Philippines established.
		Appointment of Ng Choy as unofficial member of Legislative Council.
1881	December	Visit of HRHs Albert and George aboard HMS *Bacchante*.
		Government telephone service initiated.
1882		Publication of the Chadwick Report on the sanitary conditions of Hong Kong.
1883	June	Hong Kong connected by cable to Shanghai and Foochow.
	July	Canton—Kowloon telegraph line opens.
1884	August	Sino-French War sparks riots in colony.
	October	Hong Kong Jockey Club formed.
1885		Hong Kong Government sets up Land Commission to investigate overcrowding in the City of Victoria.
1887		College of Medicine for the Chinese founded. Sun Yat-sen was an early student.
1888	May	Peak Tramway from the Cathedral to Victoria Gap opened to traffic.
1890	April	Visits of Duke and Duchess of Connaught.
		Duke lays foundation stone of Praya Reclamation initiated by Sir Paul Chater.
		Scheme to reclaim two miles of waterfront from Naval Yard to West Point initiated.
		Public telephone service offered by China and Japan Telephone Company.
1892		Gas lighting introduced in Kowloon.
1894	May	Outbreak of bubonic plague, resulting in 2,547 deaths. 80,000 flee the colony.
	June	European merchants petition Britain for constitutional reform.
		Wong Shing, second Chinese unofficial member of Legislative Council, appointed.
1895		Over 20,000 coolies strike against new lodging-house regulations.
1896		Second bubonic plague epidemic.
		Completion of Pedder's Wharf (later Blake Pier).
1897		Hong Kong Club moves to new building at present site on Jackson Road.
1898		Signing of Convention of Peking provides for 99-year lease of New Territories to Britain.
1899	April	Flag raising ceremony at Tai Po (New Territories).
		Local opposition by Chinese militia against British take-over. Chinese magistrate and militia expelled from Kowloon Walled City.
1900		Hong Kong serves as base for Chinese Expeditionary Force during Boxer Uprising.
		Chinese General Chamber of Commerce founded.
1901		Bubonic casualties re-occur—worst since 1894.
1902		Completion of Mountain Lodge, Governor's retreat on the Peak.

1904		Electric tramways on Hong Kong Island begin service.
1906	*September*	Worst typhoon recorded in Hong Kong history: casualties exceed 10,000. Sixty-one large vessels and 652 junks lost.
1907	*February*	Governor Sir Matthew Nathan succeeded by Sir Frederick Lugard.
1910	*March*	All opium divans in Hong Kong and New Territories closed. British sections of Kowloon—Canton Railway opened.
	October	First automobile in Hong Kong.
1911	*October*	Chinese section of Kowloon—Canton Railway opened for traffic. First aeroplane flight in Hong Kong at Sha Tin.
1912	*January*	Opening of the new Supreme Court.
	March	Opening of University of Hong Kong.
	July	Attempted assassination of Governor Sir Henry May.
1918	*February*	Happy Valley Racecourse fire disaster—over 600 bodies recovered.
1919	*September*	Arrival of new governor, Sir Reginald Stubbs.
1921		Visit of Crown Prince of Japan (later Emperor Hirohito). Commission of Inquiry into child labour appointed.
1922	*January*	Visit of HRH Albert, Prince of Wales on board HMS *Renown*.
1923	*May*	Cenotaph unveiled by Governor Sir Reginald Stubbs.
1925	*June*	Guangzhou-Hong Kong strike which lasted until October 1926.
	November	Arrival of new governor, Cecil Clementi. Opening of Kowloon YMCA.
1928	*December*	Opening of the Peninsula Hotel in Tsim Sha Tsui.
1929	*January*	Formal opening of first Chinese library.
	October	Broadcast studios of ZBW opened.
1930	*May*	Arrival of new governor, Sir William Peel.
	December	First commercial flight from Hong Kong to Guangzhou.
1931	*September*	Anti-Japanese riots. Hong Kong-Guangzhou trunk telephone service inaugurated.
1932		Charlie Chaplin visits Hong Kong. Launching of first vehicular ferry.
1933	*February*	George Bernard Shaw visits Hong Kong University. Hong Kong Brewery and Distillers Ltd plant opened.
1934	*February*	China Fleet Club opened.
1935	*October*	New Hongkong and Shanghai Bank building opened.

Arrival of Sir Andrew Caldecott as governor of Hong Kong.
Government Exchange Fund created.

1936 January Urban Council takes over functions of Sanitary Board.
March Arrival of Imperial Airways flying boat, carrying first airmail from Britain to Hong Kong.
September Central British School opened.
October Pan-American clipper service between US and Hong Kong inaugurated.

1937 May Passenger air service between Manila and Hong Kong started.
July Marco Polo Bridge incident in Beijing marks beginning of Sino-Japanese War.
September Bias Bay area bombarded by Japanese.
October Arrival of Governor Sir Geoffrey Northcote.
December Sham Chun (Shenzhen) bombed followed by landing of Japanese troops at Bias Bay, New Territories.

1938 January Visit by Madam Chiang Kai-shek.
February Imperial Airways plane fired on by Japanese near Hong Kong.
October Kowloon-Guangzhou road closed.
Fall of Guangzhou.
Flood of Chinese refugees enter Hong Kong.
November Visit to Hong Kong of Japanese cruiser *Myoko*.
Fall of Sham Chun (Shenzhen)

1939 January Japanese occupation of Hainan Island.
February Lo Wu bombed by Japanese, 12 killed.
June Anti-Japanese demonstrations by Hong Kong students.
July Conscription for British subjects introduced and volunteer forces strengthened.
August Registration of British women and children announced.
November 44 Vickers tanks land in Hong Kong.

1940 June General Norton becomes acting governor of Hong Kong.

1941 June Centenary of founding of colony.
September Arrival of Sir Mark Young as governor.
8 December Japanese bomb Kai Tak, cross the China border and invade Hong Kong.
18 December Japanese assault on Hong Kong Island.
25 December Governor Sir Mark Young and General C M Maltby surrender to Japanese commander at the Peninsula Hotel.

1942 January Occupation of Hong Kong by Japan commences.
February Lt General Rensuke Isogai named as Japanese governor.
Allied troops incarcerated in Argyle Street and at Sham Shui Po POW camps.
Civilians interned at Stanley Internment Camp.
Foreign Office negotiates with China over return of Hong Kong after war.

1943-4 Japanese rebuild Government House (present structure).
October Seven British civilians beheaded at Stanley Beach for possession of a radio.

1945 Allied planes bomb Hong Kong.
August F C Gimson emerges from internment to set up interim British administration.
30 August British fleet under Rear Admiral Sir Cecil Harcourt sails into Victoria Harbour to accept Japanese surrender.
15 September Local Japanese commanders formally surrender to Harcourt at Government House.

	November	T W Kwok, Chinese Special Commissioner for Hong Kong, takes up duties in Hong Kong.
		Hong Kong resumes normal trading.
1946	*May*	Population returns to pre-war level of 1.6 million.
		British Military Administration ends.
		Civil government restored with return of pre-war governor, Sir Mark Young.
		Peanut vendor riot in Kowloon—strong expression of anti-British feeling.
1947	*May*	Sir Mark Young retires and is succeeded by Sir Alexander Grantham as governor.
	December	Kowloon Walled City incident.
		Chinese Commissioner announces China had never waived right of access to Kowloon Walled City. Protests over evictions by Hong Kong Government.
1948	*January*	Agreement with China to allow Chinese maritime customs posts in Hong Kong.
	April	UK Treasury control over Hong Kong's finances ends.
1949	*April*	First double-decker bus service.
	May	Hong Kong garrison to be reinforced.
	June	Reform Club petitions governor for a directly elected Legislative Council.
	October	Communists take over Guangzhou.
		Communist forces reach Hong Kong border.
1950	*January*	Left-wing political demonstrations.
	April	China National Aviation Corporation planes held at Kai Tak.
	May	Immigration controls curbing entry of immigrants from China.
	June	Korean War begins.
	December	United States imposes embargo on selected exports to and from Hong Kong.
		Population reaches 2.5 million.
1951	*February*	China imposes controls over population movements from Guangdong Province.
		UN embargo on trade with China.
1952	*March*	Riots in Kowloon over attempt by delegation from Guangzhou to bring relief to fire victims.
	May	First post-war Urban Council elections.
	July	Chinese planes grounded at Kai Tak since 1949 returned to USA.
	September	British Government agrees to abandon proposals for political reform in Hong Kong.
	October	KMT attacks communist offices and personnel in Hong Kong.
1953	*25 December*	Squatter fire at Shek Kip Mei; 58,000 people rendered homeless.
		Public Housing programme begun.
1955	*August*	Discovery of Han Dynasty tomb at Li Cheng Uk on a housing estate site.
1956	*October*	Double Tenth riots at Sham Shui Po.
1957	*May*	Rediffusion cable television service commences.
	December	Governor Sir Alexander Grantham leaves Hong Kong.
1958	*January*	Sir Robert Black sworn in as governor.
	June	Construction of first underground pedestrian subway from Connaught Road to Star Ferry terminal.
	August	Kai Tak Airport runway completed.
		Hong Kong Tourist Association established.

1959	*November*	Government report on narcotics estimates more than 150,000 addicts.
1960	*January*	Federation of Hong Kong Industries established.
		New ferries on vehicular service between Kowloon and Hung Hom.
	November	Agreement with Guangdong provincial authorities to supply water to Hong Kong.
1961		Hong Kong population reaches 3,128,000.
1962	*February*	Influx of more than 70,000 illegal immigrants from China.
	May	Border wire barricade erected. Some 60,000 illegal immigrants caught by police and returned to China.
	November	New passenger terminal at Kai Tak Airport opened by governor.
1963	*June*	Severe drought: Hong Kong authorities brought in water by chartered tanker fleet.
	October	Chinese TV service begins.
1964	*April*	Sir David Trench became governor.
1965		Influx of US troops to Wanchai begins—to last until the end of Vietnam war.
	January	The flower *Bauhinia Blakeana* selected as the emblem of Hong Kong.
	April	Major bank runs on Canton Trust, Commercial Bank and Hang Seng Bank. Government took over management and limited withdrawals to HK$100 per day.
	June	Madame Li Shui-fu appointed first female member of Legislative Council.
1966	*March*	Ocean Terminal officially opened.
	April	Kowloon riots, sparked by proposed increase of 5 cents in first-class Star Ferry fare.
		Lion Rock Tunnel opens.
	July	Visit of The Beatles to Hong Kong.
	October	Trade Development Council created.
1967	*May*	Labour dispute at plastic flower factory at San Po Kong sparks off demonstrations, strikes, poster campaigns and placing of bombs in crowded places by left-wing sympathizers of the Cultural Revolution.
	July	Five Hong Kong policemen killed by People's Liberation Army soldiers at the border. Several incidents of abduction and imprisonment.
	November	TVB, local TV station, begins transmission in colour.
		Opening of Lion Rock Tunnel between Kowloon and Sha Tin.
		Hong Kong Government devalues the dollar by 12.87 percent to fall in line with Britain.
		Number of people in government housing reaches one million.
1968		Government decides to establish ten city district offices 'to bridge the gap between the administration and the people'.
1969	*March*	Hong Kong joins Asian Development Bank.
	September	Sha Tin designated as new satellite town in the New Territories.
1970	*April*	Arrival at Kai Tak of first Boeing 747.
	December	Visit of Pope Paul VI.
		Population reaches 4 million.
1971	*April*	Introduction of public assistance welfare scheme.
	May	Prevention of Bribery Ordinance comes into effect.
	September	Free education in government primary schools.

1972		Sir Muray MacLehose appointed as Governor.
	July	New Towns Programme officially launched.
		Large influx of Vietnamese boat people.
	October	HRH Princess Alexandra arrives in Hong Kong to open Cross Harbour Tunnel.

1974	*February*	Anti-corruption commission established (ICAC).
	November	Hong Kong dollar allowed to float against other currencies.

1975	*May*	Royal Visit—first visit of reigning monarch to Hong Kong.
		Queen Elizabeth II opens new Hung Hom railway terminus.

1976	*January*	Death of Zhou Enlai mourned in Hong Kong.

1977		Second Lion Rock Tunnel opened.

1978	*August*	Taxi strike.
	October	Opening of Sha Tin Racecourse.

1979	*September*	First MTR train runs from Shek Kip Mei to Kwun Tong.
	October	Hong Kong—Canton direct train service resumes.

1980	*October*	'Touch base' policy of allowing illegal immigrants from China to remain in Hong Kong ends.
		Population reaches 5.2 million

1982	*March*	Aberdeen—Happy Valley Road Tunnel opened.
	May	Arrival of Sir Edward Youde as governor.
	September	Mrs Margaret Thatcher, British prime minister, comes to Hong Kong and opens China Light and Power Station at Castle Peak.
		Prime Minister Thatcher visits Beijing to discuss the future of Hong Kong.
		Vietnamese boat people confined to closed areas.

1983	*July*	Completion of electrification of Kowloon—Canton Railway.
		Formal rounds of Sino-British talks begin.
	October	Hong Kong dollar linked to US dollar at conversion rate of HK$7.80 to US$1.

1984	*March*	Visit of Sir Geoffrey Howe, British foreign secretary, to Hong Kong.
	July	Sir Geoffrey Howe outlines terms of Joint Agreement.
	September	Text of Agreement initialled by British ambassador, Sir Richard Evans, in Beijing.
	November	Government issues White Paper on the Future Development of Representative Government in Hong Kong.
	December	Mrs Thatcher signs Sino-British Joint Declaration in Beijing and addresses Legislative and Executive Councils.

1985	*May*	Opening of MTR Hong Kong Island line from Admiralty to Chai Wan.
	June	Government takes over Overseas Trust Bank.
	September	Elections for 12 Legislative Council seats from the functional constituencies.
	December	Opening of the unified Stock Exchange in Exchange Square.
		New Hongkong and Shanghai Bank headquarters completed.
		Legislative Council moves into the old Supreme Court building.

1986	*January*	Joint venture contract for construction of Daya Bay nuclear power station signed.

	March	Urban Council elections.
		Government takes over Union Bank.
	April	Regional Council set up to handle municipal affairs outside the jurisdiction of Urban Council.
	October	Visit of Queen Elizabeth II and HRH Duke of Edinburgh.
	December	Death of Governor Sir Edward Youde in Beijing.
1987	*April*	Arrival of new governor, Sir David Wilson.
	July	British National (Overseas) passport introduced to replace British Dependent Territories passport.
	October	Hang Seng Index falls from 3,207 to 2,241 in one day. Hong Kong Stock Exchange closed for four days.
1988	*February*	White Paper on 'The Development of Representative Government' issued.
	March	Sir Ti Liang Yang sworn in as Hong Kong's first Chinese chief justice.
	April	Publication of consultative document on Draft Basic Law of Hong Kong's Special Administrative Region to provide mini-constitution for administration of Hong Kong after 1997.
	May	Sir Geoffrey Howe pledges British Government's commitment to full implementation of Joint Declaration.
	June	Screening of Vietnamese boat people introduced to determine whether they are genuine political refugees or economic migrants.
	July	Permanent office of Sino-British Joint Liaison Group set up in Hong Kong.
	September	Light Rail Transit System between Tuen Mun and Yuen Long opens. Elections for Legislative Council held.
	November	Governor David Wilson visits Beijing to meet Premier Li Peng and other senior Chinese officials.
1989	*March*	First group of 75 Vietnamese boat people voluntarily return to Vietnam.
	May	Government announces decision to allow entry of 3,000 skilled foreign workers.
		First series of mass rallies takes place in support of the democratic movement in China.
	June	Over one million Hong Kong people hold rallies to mourn June 4th massacre in Beijing.
	July	Sir Geoffrey Howe states in Hong Kong that Britain cannot give the right of abode in the United Kingdom to 3.25 million British Dependent Territory citizens in Hong Kong.
	September	Eastern Harbour Crossing opens to road traffic.
	October	Governor delivers annual policy speech and announces a massive Port and Airport Development Scheme costing HK$127 billion.
	November	The Prince and Princess of Wales arrive for a four-day visit. Their programme included the official opening of the new Cultural Centre and Convention Centre.
	December	Li Kwan-ha became the first local officer appointed Commissioner of Police.
		First mandatory repatriation to Hanoi of 51 Vietnamese boat people screened out as economic migrants.
		British Government announces that 225,000 people or 50,000 heads of households in Hong Kong will be granted full British passports.
1990	*January*	Governor Sir David Wilson leaves for Beijing for discussions on Hong Kong with Chinese Prime Minister Li Peng.
		Foreign Secretary Douglas Hurd visits the territory for the first time.
	4 April	Basic Law for the Special Administrative Region of Hong Kong promulgated by the National People's Congress in Beijing, to come into effect 1 July 1997.
		The Minister of State with special responsibilty for Hong Kong, Mr Francis Maude, arrives for a five-day visit.

May	The Governor welcomes the decision by US President Bush to maintain China's Most Favoured Nation status (yet to be accepted by US government).	
August	Hong Kong implements trade and economic sanctions against Iraq and Kuwait	
September	Visit of the new Minister of State with special responsibility for Hong Kong, Lord Caithness.	
	Britain, Vietnam and Hong Kong agree to repatriate boat people who, while not volunteering to return, are not opposed to going back.	
October	The government announces that it will finance the construction of the Lantau Fixed Crossing leading to the new Chek Lap Kok airport.	
	Governor visits Europe to strengthen ties with the European Community.	
November	Governor visits Japan to boost bilateral trade.	
December	Application period begins for British citizenship under the British Nationality (Hong Kong) Act.	
	Governor visits London for discussions with the new Prime Minister, Mr John Major.	
	The Hongkong and Shanghai Banking Corporation announces its intended re-organisation under a British-based holding company.	

1991   4 July   Agreement to the Memorandum of Understanding between the British and Chinese Governments (to be signed later this year) gives the official go ahead on the new airport project at Chek Lap Kok, Lantau.

Introduction

Victoria, Hong Kong, in April 1841 before the town was built (right)

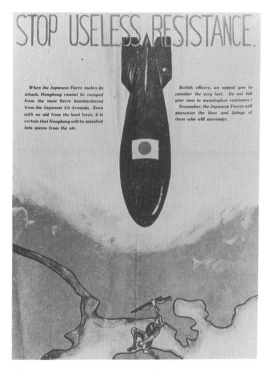

Leaflets dropped on Hong Kong by Japanese bombers to show the futility of Allied resistance. The writing on the leaflet reads as follows:

When the Japanese Force makes its attack, Hongkong cannot be escaped from the most fierce bombardment from the Japanese Air Armada.Even with no aid from the land force, it is certain that Hongkong will be smashed into pieces from the air. British officers, we appeal you to consider the very fact. Do not kill your men in meaningless resistance! Remember, the Japanese Forces will guarantee the lives and livings of those who will surrender *(above).*

First, I must emphasize that this is above all an illustrated history of Hong Kong. The commentaries are not intended to present a straightforward chronological account of Hong Kong, but rather are a set of personal observations that serve as a connecting thread for the imperial history of the colony. Hong Kong was ceded by China to Great Britain after the military and naval defeats of the Opium Wars (1839-42). In the succeeding 150 years it has become one of the world's most important trading centres with a population of some six million people, most of whom are descended from Mainland Chinese migrants.

As many writers have pointed out, Hong Kong has never fitted neatly into the British colonial scheme for the development of overseas territories. Despite its growth and arguable social maturity, the inescapable Chinese connection hindered it from aspiring to national independence and self-government. Yet there has been a remarkable fusion of Chinese and British cultural values interacting with one another to produce a miraculous offspring: capitalism. As Jan Morris, travel writer and historian, has observed: 'Opportunism is the *raison d'être* of Hong Kong, and virtually every private citizen of this colony is a speculator and a capitalist, from the richest developer to the poorest labourer. Making money is the purpose of Hong Kong.'

Hong Kong was afforded an unusual opportunity to exploit the traditional Chinese virtues of industry, thrift and resilience during the paralysing early years of the People's Republic of China after 1949. With a symbiosis of Western business organization and Chinese entrepreneurial spirit, Hong Kong rapidly outdistanced Shanghai and, to a lesser degree, other treaty ports such as Guangzhou (Canton), despite having to overcome a fundamental geographical disadvantage—while both Shanghai and Guangzhou were able to tap the rich natural resources of vast hinterlands, Hong Kong, during its first 100 years as a British trading depot, was notorious for its meagre physical disposition as 'a bare, barren rock'. Its only apparent asset was a series of harbours sheltered from the typhoons of the South China Sea.

Formally, Hong Kong became a British colony in 1843, with a governor and an administrative apparatus similar to other British possessions of that time, and with a Legislative Council of officials that included a chief justice and a military commander-in-chief. Yet despite the imposition of a British administrative and legal system, colonial policy meant adapting British conventions and customs to local ways. For example, the Chinese custom that permitted a man to have several legal wives was not outlawed until well into the twentieth century. By the same token, the 'Chineseness' of Hong Kong has been influenced by Western values to produce a complex, subtle amalgam of behaviour. It could be said that there has been in Hong Kong a true marriage of Confucian values and British colonial ethics. Indeed, the application of the principles of nineteenth-century *laissez faire* and, in more recent times, positive non-intervention by the Hong Kong Government has provided an ideal environment for business, and thus for Hong Kong as a whole, to prosper. However, instead of taking on a more cosmopolitan internationalism like Singapore, Hong Kong has remained a distinctly Chinese city, whilst demonstrating its willingness to adapt itself to changing circumstances and markets.

The first section of this book is devoted to colonial Hong Kong, starting from the First Opium War, when Jardine, Matheson and Company realized its objective of establishing a trading depot in South China. Although Hong Kong's cession was treated separately from Chinese concessions in the five treaty ports— Shanghai, Ningpo (Ningbo), Amoy (Xiamen), Foochow (Fuzhou) and Canton (Guangzhou)—it functioned in essentially the same way, as a port and a base for the commercial penetration of Qing-dynasty China by European shippers and traders. These were the days of 'pomp and circumstance', reflecting the British imperial presence: the royal visitations, the locally-recruited defence force on parade, the arrivals and departures of successive governors in their cockatoo-plumed helmets and starched white uniforms.

The illusory military supremacy of Britain in the Far East came to an end with the onset of World War II and the decisive Japanese victories in Hong Kong and Southeast Asia, the subject of Part Two. Even though their victories were soon reversed, the Japanese—who saw their role as an Asiatic liberator of Asian peoples from Western imperialism—won for their victims (if not for themselves) a lasting triumph. From 1945 onwards the right of the indigenous people in the region to self-determination and independence could no longer be entirely suppressed by notions of Western superiority.

Part Three describes Hong Kong's subsequent emergence from the ruins of war with a new and vital economy. Its harbour was transformed from a depot for the coastal trade of China and Southeast Asia into a truly international port and a manufacturing centre, producing an increasingly diverse range of light-industrial products— textiles, clothing, plastics, watches and electronics—to name just a few. Since Hong Kong produced no raw materials (as the city grew it could not even feed itself), the vital ingredient for its success was the enterprise and business acumen of its traders, who created new industries and carved out new markets in almost every country of the world.

The 'new' Hong Kong treated in Part Four has been a place of ever-increasing prosperity, some of which has percolated down to the poorer socio-economic stratum of society. The result is a city of considerable diversification and sophistication. Physically, a different Hong Kong has come into being. Glittering

Calendar for 'Camel' brand paints, Hong Kong products of the 1950s

glass-walled skyscrapers are intersected by arterial roads and tunnels; underground railways have made the sedan chairs and tree-lined pavements obsolete. The farmers of the paddy-fields of the New Territories have all but disappeared, now replaced by the stalagmite growth of the new towns.

Contemporary view from the Peak looking towards Tsim Sha Tsui

Governing this vastly increased metropolis has become much more complex as the government has had to assume more responsibilities than providing rudimentary shelter, law and order. Since the 1970s, it has been actively involved in promoting a dynamic concept of the quality of life, expressed in better public health and living conditions, more diverse leisure and educational facilities and a different, if not less polluted, physical environment. Even in its economic and social policies, the administration has moved away from the *laissez faire* economic abstractions of Sir John Cowperthwaite, Hong Kong's financial secretary during the 1960s. Some provision is now made for the infirm, the aged and to some extent, the unemployed.

Although a fully democratic system of government is now ruled out, the crisis of the 1980s and 1990s over the future of Hong Kong has hastened some changes in the administration. Areas of the territory are now 'governed' through District Boards, whose members are elected from amongst local politicians—a proposition previously unimaginable. Yet what this is leading up to is unclear. On the one hand the capitalist infrastructure of law and political freedom is seen as a prerequisite for Hong Kong's investments and profits which will benefit the Motherland—China. On the other hand, socialist ideology is still far from dead on the Mainland, where economic reforms have been tempered by the leadership's insistence that there is to be no abandonment of the egalitarian principles implicit in Chinese-style socialism.

The imminence of the Chinese take-over in 1997 has sent a decisive shock-wave through the colonial city-state. One question is ever-present in people's minds: Can Hong Kong, as it is today, survive the inescapable changes which must take place? These changes will permeate the structure of Hong Kong as a whole, not just the political and administrative framework. One interesting case in point is language. Colloquial Cantonese and colonial English have long overshadowed the national language of China, Mandarin, or *Putonghua*, which the local population views as somewhat remote. Now, with 1997 looming ahead, patriotic local teachers are insisting that Mandarin should be taught in Hong Kong's schools as a means of inculcating students with a sense of Chinese heritage. Clearly the teaching of Mandarin is a necessity with the return to China; but what place is there for Mandarin, if any, in a city nurtured on economic internationalism? Do the people of Hong Kong belong to China, or to the wider world?

In this connection, Jan Morris has posed a question about the character and fate of not just the 'colonial' cities of the world: Do the major world cities have destinies, an exponential of growth and decay? Hong Kong clearly does have such a destiny in political terms. The end to British rule in June 1997 is that bench mark. But before that crucial metamorphosis takes place, it is instructive to consider Hong Kong's history as a British dependency. It is that over-arching view which is presented in *The Colony That Never Was.*

THE COLONIAL CITY
A Description of Victoria in the 1860s

As we steamed up the harbour, the town of Victoria came into view, stretching along the foot of these mountains for a distance of more than four miles, if you begin at the Chinese town and measure up to Jardine's at East Point; then there are terraces rising over each other up the steep hillsides, and villa residences large and small standing in well laid-out compounds, and built in the best English style.

About half-way down the town, but high on the hill, stands Government House, a handsome building, the Bishop's residence lower down, to which is attached a Chinese College, marked by a small round tower.

The Barracks are of course low down, in a most hot and unhealthy position, and the Commander-in-Chief's house above the Barracks, but still not well placed. Then close to the main wharf on the left is Dent's house . . . the Club House, a convenient building, faces the Post Office in the centre of the town in Queen's Road; as you land at Pedder's Wharf and walk up the short distance from the water to Queen's Road, the right leads you towards the Chinese town, the left to the Barracks and the English quarter, but the chief family residences are on the side of the hill which is tastefully planted.

Rev R J L McGhee

*T*he list of old buildings in Hong Kong is longer than one suspects, despite the many instances where the nineteenth-century structures have been replaced by the sparkling buildings of modern Hong Kong. Here four examples spring to mind: the Hongkong and Shanghai Bank building, the Hong Kong Club, Murray House and the Repulse Bay Hotel.

Murray House once stood at the foot of Garden Road, opposite the former Military Parade Ground where the Hilton Hotel now stands. Designed by a Royal Engineer as the Sergeants' Mess, it was a prime example of the military architecture during the founding period of Hong Kong. Its low verandahs and classical columns made it a unique example of a barrack as well as a powerful reminder of the planning involved in the foundation of the colony. The site where it stood is now occupied by another monument, the Bank of China tower designed by I M Pei, the Chinese-American architect.

The second example of official coolness in Hong Kong's colonial buildings is the Repulse Bay Hotel, once the epitome of the British Empire. When local conservationists were protesting against the demolition of the original building, the administrator responsible declared the edifice to be of no historical significance.

Hong Kong cannot escape its colonial heritage, even though the local authorities have sometimes tried to forget or even obliterate it. Despite rapid commercial development in Hong Kong, a nucleus of colonial buildings still exists in Victoria. Government House (where the governor resides) and the Government Offices, the Cathedral and the Bishop's House still stand at this symbolic junction of Church and State.

The most important fossil of the colonial age in Hong Kong is the Legislative Council Building, a modern structure with a classical appearance that was formerly the Supreme Court. The court vacated its old site for a high-rise building in Wan Chai. In its new role as the

*The facade of the first City Hall, opened in 1869 (preceding page);
the old Praya in the late nineteenth century (above); the Bank of China and
the Hongkong and Shanghai Bank buildings, at the time of the Coronation
of Queen Elizabeth II, 1953 (below)*

seat of the legislature, with (it is hoped) an added constitutional significance in the future Special Administrative Region, it will perhaps remain a 'timeless' building in pristine state.

Reclamation has had a profound effect on north Hong Kong Island. Early photographs show davits hung on the harbour-facing walls of the old Hongkong Bank building holding dinghies ready to be rowed out to ships in the harbour. Also, westward along the waterfront towards the site of the old Post Office (now Worldwide House), there was a creek running up to Pedder Street, in the present-day heart of Central District. The winding upper reaches of Queen's Road Central mark the general line of the north shore of Hong Kong Island before reclamation.

Reclamation, so necessary for expansion beyond the confines of the island's littoral, began with the commencement of commercial development. A prime example of this is the site of the Jardine establishment (next to the Excelsior Hotel), originally standing on the waterfront at Causeway Bay, but now located quite a distance inshore. Recently the governor mentioned in his address to the Legislative Council that the new Convention Centre, itself sited on reclaimed land at Wan Chai, would very soon be 300 metres inland from the waterfront.

The result of so much reclamation, still being energetically carried out past the Macau Ferry Terminal and towards the western tip of Hong Kong Island, has been to provide the foundations of the ever-growing Central district.

This original waterfront was the main business venue in the nineteenth century. Here were the docks and quays for the famous clippers and the temporary barracks for the infamous coolie trade. But despite redevelopment, the centre of gravity of the port remains where it was during the last century. It is the arteries of transportation which have changed.

They originally ran between the merchants' residences at the base of the Peak and the harbour. Today the main thoroughfare is Garden Road, but in the past the military enclave stood in the way and the route for the sedan-chair bearers and rickshaw coolies skirted a gaol (now next to the Central Police Station) and continued down Arbuthnot Road to the famous ladder streets. These ladder streets, constructed of slabs of granite, still lead to the Central Market. Hong Kong was a pedestrians' town, even if the more fortunate were borne over this rocky terrain in their sedan chairs.

The central business district is like a narrow ribbon running along the new waterfront. The traffic has now been re-routed along the new waterfront highway in a series of under- and over-passes which fly over the old commercial heart of this district, Western District. This is still pre-eminently the home of the Chinese businesses.

The commercial district has always been congested, in contrast to the official enclaves which were given that valuable commodity— space, although they do look a little cramped nowadays. This is true for Flagstaff House, Government House, the Cathedral and the older sections of the government administrative offices.

Colonial Hong Kong in its heyday was a surprisingly elegant place, with its Italianate clubs and country houses. But the commercial hongs and shipping offices depended heavily upon the labours of the energetic poor. A closer look would reveal tightly-packed Chinese bazaars and ragged, scantily-fed coolies; wharf labourers running along the praya with their poles balancing heavy loads of cargo across their bony shoulders; rickshaw-pullers, sedan-chair bearers and immigrants were forced to live and sleep on the pavements. These people made up the bulk of the 'home-

less' who lived outside the foreigners' colon-naded buildings.

Today the colonial city is a vertical city, congested and even choked with motor vehicles; but socially, it is more homogeneous. The contrasts between wealth and poverty are less extreme and less visible.

The Repulse Bay Hotel, sketched by Mel Harris, 1982

PART ONE

Where the Sun Never Sets
Hong Kong 1841-1941

A little England in the Eastern Seas, the creation of British energy, enterprise and industry.

J M Dalton, London, 1886.

There is a strange symmetry in the history of Hong Kong. The years 1984–1997, Hong Kong's last years as a British territory, are a run-up to retrocession by China. This period of disengagement at the end of the British chapter of Hong Kong's history is paralleled by a symmetrical phase of ambiguous association at the beginning of the nineteenth century, before Britain's occupation of Hong Kong in 1841.

The Canton System was the keyhole through which the Qing authorities gave foreign merchants indirect, limited and seasonal access to trade with China. But in the early nineteenth century it had gone through several crises, particularly following clashes between the mandarin magistrates—the upholders of Chinese laws and customs—and the captains and supercargoes of the East-India men that traded at the southern port. To the presidents of the Select Committee of the East India Company in Macau, setting up 'a convenient station on the Eastern Coast of China', free from the restraints and extortions of the mandarins was a matter of great urgency. An island base for trade was a logical solution to the problems of interference. [1]

Badge of the Colony of Hong Kong designed in 1869 (above);

Messrs Jardine and Matheson, c 1832 (below)

Amidst speculation as to the best location for such a base, the affirmation of the China trader, Alexander Matheson, in the *Canton Register* for 1836, was to be decisive. He thundered: 'If the lion's paw is to be put down on any part of the south side of China, let it be in Hong Kong.' It was Jardine, Matheson and Company who transferred their godowns and counting houses from Macau to Hong Kong in 1841, and who built up the most impressive commercial establishment on the island. From their base at East Point (modern Causeway Bay), they anticipated and outshone the official cantonment of military and administrative officials in the Central and Western districts of the island. Indeed, they were the founders of Hong Kong even before the ratification of a formal treaty. Such a treaty would involve a war with China and prolonged diplomatic negotiations and conclude in victorious naval engagements in the Pearl River estuary.

Settling for the predominantly hilly Hong Kong Island as a base for the penetration of China by Western commerce was nevertheless somewhat problematic. Author G R Sayer summed this up well: '. . . the peninsula of Kowloon [on the opposite shore of the harbour] . . . from the earliest days of the colony, looked alluring to Hong Kong residents, who contrasted its southern aspect and its comfortable recumbent spread with their own stiff and upright posture on the island's northern slopes . . .' [2]

At that time, the shores of Kowloon were still potentially hostile areas. In 1839, when the armada of Royal Navy ships and merchantmen had sheltered in Hong Kong waters during the stormy years of the first Opium War, an insignificant battle took place there. The Chinese troops stationed in their decrepit forts on Tsim Sha Tsui

Seafight between Government gunboats and pirates, artist unknown (left); figurehead from a wrecked opium ship of the Jardine fleet (right)

Point, where modern Kowloon begins, were routed. Despite its proximity to the infant settlement, the presence of the enemy, so weak at that time, was not considered a real threat.

The British, then in virtual possession of the island, took the matter further. As *The Chinese Account of the Opium War* recounts: 'The Co-Hong merchants being unwilling to go to Hong Kong on account of the perils of the Sea [even to take what is now the short Star Ferry ride] . . . it was proposed to exchange Hong Kong for Tsim Sha Chou [sic] Point and Kowloon.'

We do not know if this was a serious suggestion or who proposed it. But when the commercial prospects of Hong Kong did not live up to expectations in those early years, nearby Kowloon seemed an inviting place. These greener pastures were to be, of course, the next instalment in the extension of Hong Kong. In 1858 it became a military encampment for combined Anglo-French operations in Guangdong Province and North China.

Unlike the 99-year lease on the New Territories (signed in 1898), the terms for the acquisition of the Kowloon Peninsula were converted from a lease arrangement, originally made in 1858, to an outright cession with the signing of the Treaty of Tientsin (Tianjin) in the same year. Hong Kong's current situation might have occurred four decades earlier.

The tenuous, even precarious, existence Hong Kong led in its early years, was due to conditions never to be completely dispelled.[3] A little-known episode illustrates this state of impermanence. In February 1841, the entire settlement was relocated with the resumption of hostilities against China. It is reported that on this occasion, as a safeguard, the camps and bivouacs ashore were transferred to the remote island of Saw Chau off Lantau. The British flag, only just hoisted by Commodore Sir J J Gordon Bremer at Possession Point on 26 January, was hauled down 'as it was impossible to spare a sufficient number of troops to garrison it', according to Commander Bingham. This short but significant interlude lasted about one month until the commodore of the Naval Expedition had returned to Hong Kong waters and the

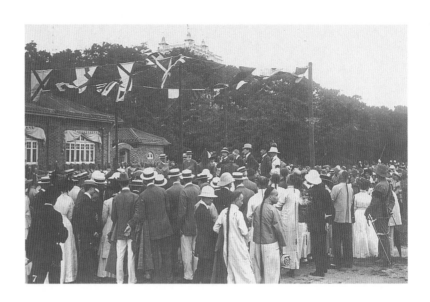

Campaign medals awarded to Allied
Expeditionary Forces for battles in the First
and Second Opium Wars (above);
opening of the Kowloon—Canton Railway,
1910 (right)

City of Victoria resumed its erratic performance on the stage of East Asian politics.

Here let us consider briefly the question of opium, the commodity which was largely responsible for the creation of Hong Kong as an outpost of the British Empire. Moreover, it is the one article of trade, coloured by moral censure and eventual international condemnation, which gave substance to Chinese claims that the British occupation of Hong Kong and its adjoining territories was an insult, physical and psychological, to be suffered temporarily until its yoke could be cast off.

When British and American traders began doing business with China it was still a mercantilist age, when economists focused closely upon the crude balance of trade. As the growing attraction of Chinese commodities—silk, tea and other exotica—swelled the bill of imports into Europe, it was understandable that merchants should seek an article for Chinese consumption. This should be obtainable preferably in large quantities only from abroad, in order to command a ready sale. Attempts to ship cotton and other textiles—products of the Industrial Revolution—were to no avail. Quite possibly it was not the Western traders, looking for shipments to pay for their outward cargoes from Guangzhou, who introduced the drug to China, but rather the Chinese merchants themselves. They sold the opium in Batavia, the former Dutch East Indies, as early as the eighteenth century. They would not have confined themselves to shipping directly from Turkey or India, but, ever eager to gain profits from their trading activities, they would surely have brought cargoes to Guangzhou.

This is not to deny that the economic foundations of Hong Kong were built upon opium. For there it was, laid up in hulks off East Point, instead of in Lintin, the former opium depot in the Pearl River estuary. [4] Hong Kong grew commercially by engaging in smuggling, while successfully keeping at a distance the parasites of prosperity—the pirates who abounded in the waters around Hong Kong. This combination of licit and illicit activities has continued in varying degrees until the present day, with the traffic both various and often two-way. In more recent times silver dollars, illegal immigrants and drugs have been shipped into Hong Kong, while salt, petroleum, cigarettes, automo-

Hong Kong ferry terminal, Blake's pier, 1930

biles, luxury items and electronic goods have found their way out of the commodity-rich entrepôt to China.

The caravaners who flocked to the safety of Hong Kong in 1839 formed a ramshackle encampment on the southern shore of the harbour. Even Hong Kong's first governor, Sir Henry Pottinger, apparently lived *al fresco* in a tent on the beach until more permanent lodgings could be rented for him. It was not until 1855 that the seat of His Excellency Her Majesty's Representative in the colony was securely fixed to the spot where Government House now stands. It is a domain which once included the grounds of the present Botanical Gardens and swept down to the harbour. Such a commanding position has now been eroded by the growth of the Central district.

In 1842, when the city of Queenstown (Pottinger named the city Victoria in 1843) stretched about four miles along the northern shoreline of the island, it was recorded that brick buildings were 'fast rising'. The rest were mat sheds, bound by a fragile cladding on bamboo framing. Even the first Anglican church was constructed in such material until it was blown down during a typhoon.[5]

But it was in the Chinese bazaars, Upper and Lower, where an opportunist army of camp followers, army and navy suppliers, and others anxious to cater to the needs of the newly arrived residents formed the free-wheeling 'local' Chinese business communities.

In 1841, it was estimated that the local inhabitants of Hong Kong numbered about 15,000. They were mostly labourers and fishermen, plus a fair number from Chekchu (Stanley) who combined these pursuits with offshore piratical activities. By 1845, this population had grown to 23,817, and by 1850 to over 30,000.

This community, which the latter-day missionary, Dr Eitel,[6] considered to be the dregs of Chinese society, did not for the most part settle permanently but maintained their ancestral homes in China. Until the 1850s these temporary residents travelled back and forth, riding the tides of business—and patriotism. In 1856 a second chapter of Western conflict with China began over the *Arrow* incident. This affair represented Hong Kong's attempts to assert itself against the Chinese dues and official controls which were designed to dampen the

Sun Yat-sen, President of China, with a group of students outside the University of Hong Kong, February 1923

free trade status secured by the Treaty of Nanking. Local inhabitants were ordered to bring down Hong Kong by boycott, exodus, arson and the mass poisoning of bread, the European residents' staple food.

This was not the only problem. In Britain *The Times* (15 March 1859) noted that 'Hong Kong [was] always connected with some fatal pestilence, some doubtful war, or some discreditable internal squabble'. Indeed, the major hazard to the British military stationed on the island was the prevalence of tropical fevers—malaria, ague and cholera in particular—which decimated the garrison's regiments until the swamps and nullahs were drained in the 1850s. These dangers to the health of Hong Kong's inhabitants led to further suggestions to abandon the place for a more salubrious location.

China, too, had problems. But these were indirectly to benefit Hong Kong. In the 1850s, China suffered civil wars, and an estimated 15 million people were slaughtered during the unprecedented bloodletting following the defeat of the Taiping Rebellion. Hong Kong now experienced its first fruitful influx of refugees to bolster the population and stimulate its economy.

Regardless of ideological sacrifices, the population of Hong Kong swelled. So far as the official censuses allow us to estimate, between the years 1859 and 1865 (the climax of the Taiping tragedy) the actual number of people in Hong Kong exceeded 100,000 for the first time; government revenues increased by 300 percent.

The larger population sparked off business activity and prosperity but it also brought social problems, mainly related to sanitation and public health. The settlement had previously consisted of separate cantonments—one military, one 'native' and one official—which were linked by European merchants, their Portuguese clerks and the well-to-do Chinese compradors. With more crowded conditions, disease spread quickly. The military already suffered badly from the rigours of the climate despite medical attention and isolation. The Chinese who had settled here had their own effective traditional herbal remedies, and may have benefitted from greater natural immunity to local diseases.

In the 1880s particularly, the problem worsened. The City of Victoria, the core of Hong Kong Island, began to merge these separate enclaves of culture and environment. Overcrowding resulted, Hong Kong became prone to epidemics, and the very viability of the place came under threat.

The government was in a quandary; it did not want to depend too much upon local ratepayers—the up-and-coming rich Chinese merchant class—to implement public health schemes, nor did it want matters to get out of hand. The European merchants, who were most anxious about their health, were in a minority, and the government had to tread warily.

But Hong Kong underwent the same sanitary investigations as the industrial cities of nineteenth-century Britain. Osbert Chadwick, son of the great British municipal reformer Edwin Chadwick, was sent out to Hong Kong by the Colonial Office, once in 1882 and again in 1920.

His first report took full measure of the problem, a rootless, overcrowded population unconcerned with public health, and recommended the Sanitary Movement solutions: a clean,

uncontaminated water supply, glazed earthenware pipes for sewage disposal and, ultimately, better housing.

Posters of the 1925 Hong Kong—Canton strike boycott

A Sanitary Board, set up in 1883 and reorganised in 1887, would supply the administrative machinery for safeguarding the health of Hong Kong. Municipal reform was shelved and another 50 years were to pass before the Urban Council emerged from its chrysalis. Though, let it be said, that neglected creature has never been allowed to develop into a fully-fledged system of municipal government for Hong Kong.

It took another visitation of the dreaded bubonic plague in 1894 to remove some of the obstacles which prevented the rapid implementation of Chadwick's remedies for insanitary Hong Kong. The plague baccillus was an international export, carried by fleas on black rats from port to port across the Pacific. Some form of quarantine was needed; in some cases the ships bringing the cargoes to those ports were refused entry. The problem had to be dealt with thoroughly and expeditiously to prevent the plague from spreading further.

At that time there was no cure or inoculation for plague. Even the traditional Chinese prophylactic measures offered little hope of recovery to victims. And local residents were suspicious of the British sanitary inspectors and troops, who had the job of disinfecting, demolishing and burning the infected premises, most of which were located in the old bazaar area of Taipingshan. Thousands of them took the first opportunity to flee to the relative safety of nearby Guangzhou.

Aware that cultural differences in treating the pestilence might arouse fervid opposition to official actions, the Sanitary Board, nevertheless, had to enforce its draconian measures. Landlords and tenants were given 48 hours to clean up their properties, and any building considered to be unfit for human habitation would be evacuated. In all, 350 houses in Taipingshan, Central district, were condemned and demolished. Leaders of the local Chinese community, such as Dr Ho Kai, felt such measures to be an affront to their susceptibilities; but there were some material benefits—some of the notorious rookeries

March and October issues of 'Tavern Topics',
published by the Hongkong and Shanghai
Hotels Ltd. in the 1930s (above and far right)

were rebuilt in Hong Kong's first inner-city urban renewal programmes. The plague eventually went away, but it returned later that year and each summer until 1921.

Britain was to take advantage of the weakness of the Qing dynasty in its decline and negotiate for another extension of its Hong Kong possessions in 1898. When the New Territories, consisting of over 90,000 hectares, was added to the peninsular territory of Kowloon (as far north as what is now known as Boundary Street), the island depot and trading post was effectively transformed into a concession like Shanghai. This huge hinterland of mountains and paddy-fields was a strategic buffer zone, but it only became economically viable as a result of the extended urbanization of Hong Kong and Kowloon in the New Towns Programme of the 1970s.

There was, nevertheless, the plan to launch a rail link from the tip of the Kowloon Peninsula to the Yangtze River. Although this link was not completed until 1937, the Kowloon—Canton Railway was opened for traffic from Hong Kong in 1912. It was not a great success at first; subject to floods and attacks by bandits, it could not really compete with the diverse forms of water transport already available to Guangzhou and its surrounding markets.

Another consequence of the lease was the substantial expansion of the outer limits of the harbour. Previously the western boundary had only extended as far as Stonecutters Island near Sham Shui Po in the west, and to Kowloon City, near to the future Kai Tak Airport, in the east. The present-day configuration of air transport, industrial, shipping and residential locations was beginning to take shape.

This pattern was further consolidated with the series of harbourside reclamations on the north shore of the island and on the east and west shores of the Kowloon Peninsula, culminating in the Praya East Reclamation, proposed by Sir Paul Chater in the later part of the nineteenth century, but not completed until 1929. At the same time, the island could now be supplied with water from the New Territories via a cross-harbour pipeline.

Hong Kong and Kowloon had been linked by the cross-harbour ferries since 1880; by 1920 there was talk of the need for a cross-harbour tunnel to link the island and the burgeoning Kowloon residential and industrial districts.

The longest-standing and most contentious problem resulting from Hong Kong's situation on the doorstep of Mainland China, was the interference of the Qing Dynasty imperial authorities in the economic life of the colony. This had been an issue ever since the signing of the treaty of 1842. The Guangzhou authorities did not attach the same meaning to the words of the treaty, with regard to the imposition of tariffs on Hong Kong's entrepôt trade, as did Captain Elliot, despite the clarification of the Supplementary Treaty of the Bogue (8 October 1843): 'All persons . . . who may wish to convey goods from any one of the five ports . . . to Hong Kong, for sale or consumption, shall be at full and perfect liberty to do so . . .' This was the British determination, interpretation and intention; but geographically and fiscally, Chinese customs officials could put a stranglehold on Hong Kong's trade with the rest of China.

There was a determination, too, on the part of the Hong Kong authorities to make Hong Kong a respectable and commercial city in contrast to its previous reputation as the regional centre of smuggling, in particular of opium. Britain held the whip over China militarily, and could secure handsome instalments of compensation from merchants and the government alike for the inconvenience of the two Opium Wars (six million dollars in 1842 and eight million taels of silver in 1860); it also considered it proper to restrain the buccaneering propensities of its own pioneer traders.

Nevertheless, the Chinese revenue cruisers sailed in and out of Hong Kong waters with impunity, collecting tolls and dues from the local fishermen and junk captains. Governor Macdonnell in the 1860s was further worried by the setting up of a ring of Chinese customs ports on the Kowloon side of the harbour. [7]

Objections from the Hong Kong merchants resulted in a Chinese blockade lasting for about a quarter of a century. This historical problem was officially settled in 1886 by a Joint Sino-British Commission. But in practical terms, it was the removal of the border from Deep Bay to Mirs Bay, the northern limit of the newly-leased territory, which eased the problem.

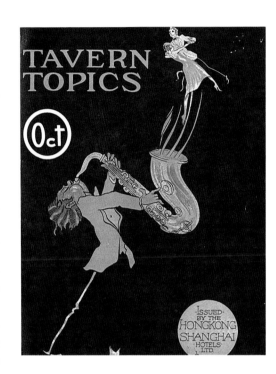

There was confidence in Hong Kong at the beginning of the twentieth century. Even the 99-year term of the lease was regarded by Hong Kong's citizens as being equivalent to eternity. The threat of China (and more ominously, of Japan) was either dismissed or ignored.

The problem of Chinese politics spilling over into the territory could not always be ignored. Hong Kong has not always been hospitable to Chinese attempts to reform or overthrow the decadent dynasty. Indeed, the most prominent Chinese revolutionary, Sun Yat-sen, had been nurtured and educated at the colony's College of Medicine for the Chinese, established in 1887. Throughout his revolutionary career, chequered by repression and defeat, Dr Sun had a close connection with Hong Kong until he died in 1925. But at a time when he was living anonymously in Central, and then with fellow-plotters in a remote farmhouse at Hung Lau, near Tuen Mun in the New Territories, the Hong Kong Government issued an interdiction against his presence in the colony. Dr Sun and his revolutionary party eventually came to the fore with the birth of the Republic of China in 1911.

It was significant that in 1912, one year after the Chinese Republic was founded, an attempt, the only one in the history of the colony, was made to assassinate the governor. The new incumbent, Sir Henry May, had just set foot on the island when the unthinkable happened. The inaugural celebrations were shattered by the crack of a would-be assassin's revolver.

Sir Henry was a brave man and not one to be outfaced by the threat of violence. Indeed, his stern authority, derived from his days as Hong Kong's superintendent of police, was to be exercised again very shortly afterwards.

The problem proved to be, as was often the case in Hong Kong, a monetary one. The colony's own currency was being swamped by sub-standard coins from Guangdong. In 1912, the Hong Kong Tramway Company refused to accept these tokens of Chinese sovereignty as its fares. The patriotism of the Wan Chai populace was deeply affronted, so they resorted to the age-old and effective Chinese weapon of boycotting the tramway. The governor stepped in, and persuaded the Legislative Council to pass a Boycott Prevention Bill. It was, without doubt, a draconian measure: entire Chinese neighbourhoods would be liable to a collective fine and imprisonment if their inhabitants refused to ride on the trams and pay for their fares in the currency of the realm. It was the kind of measure an occupying army might use to enforce its will, and it worked. The Chinese members of the Legislative Council were persuaded by the governor to take a tram ride through Hong Kong's most populous suburb alongside the harbour. The boycott ended a few days later.

In the 1920s the shadow of an even greater ideological threat hung over Hong Kong. This was international communism, or Bolshevism, as it was known at the time. Governors of Hong Kong in that decade, such as Clementi, a man sensitive to Chinese culture and traditions, urged the Colonial Office in London to get the Foreign Office (which dealt with the Chinese Government) to take effective measures to eradicate this threat; imperial capitalism in the Far East was at stake. But his appeal failed.

Matters were not helped by the fact that the virtually autonomous Guangdong Provincial Government in southern China was sympathetic to these revolutionary movements. Indeed, these nationalist, radical and socialist demonstrations of worker strength were seen by the Hong Kong Government as a deliberate attempt to bring Hong Kong down as a British colony.

Ho Chi Minh, the youthful revolutionary Vietnamese leader, 1930

1921 saw the first major crisis of industrial relations. Skilled workers, engineers and fitters from the largest industrial concerns in Hong Kong, the Taikoo Dockyard and the Hong Kong Electric Company, joined forces against an unprecedented increase in the cost of living and accommodation. Managements were then politely approached by their staff for a 40-percent increase in wages. This request met a not-altogether unexpected resistance from the employers. The result was a victory for the unions. The Fitters' Strike, as author and former colonial official Austin Coates commented, 'was a genuine Hong Kong affair'.

However, in the following year, industrial tension flared up again in the colony. The Hoi Yuen (Seamen's Union)—described by Austin Coates as 'a cross between a communist cell and an old-fashioned Chinese secret society'—came out into the open against the two most powerful shipping companies, Jardine and Matheson, and Butterfield and Swire. Another demand for a 40-percent increase in pay was made. This was seen by the shipping interests as blackmail, and the conflict soon escalated. Hundreds of ships manned by Chinese crews lay idle in the harbour; such was the strength of the Guangzhou-based union, that the strike spread to other ports in the region—including Shanghai and Bangkok, which were serviced by these European firms.

The strike also spread to the other trades servicing the European inhabitants of the colony. There was a general exodus of the local population to Guangzhou, forcing the governor to issue a proclamation forbidding exit from Hong Kong without permission. To contain the struggle, the train service to Tai Po in the New Territories was suspended, whereupon the strikers and their sympathizers fought a pitched battle with the police in an attempt to break the cordon sealing off Hong Kong from China.

There was further violence, intimidation and exaggerated sensitivity to official intervention. A stevedore, Jack A Tai, was murdered in Statue Square. E R Hallifax, the registrar general responsible for Chinese community affairs in the colony, and thereby the most prominent colonial official in Chinese eyes, mindlessly tore down a striker's placard in the heat of the struggle.

Such an attack on Chinese pride could only be reconciled by the humiliation of the government. The unfortunate Hallifax, acting on behalf of the governor, personally had to replace the sign in its original position. Summing up this three-month affair, Austin Coates wrote: 'In fact, never before or since has the government of Hong Kong quite so lost face as on that occasion.'

But the next round in the fight between Chinese radicalism and colonial capitalism, which took place three years later in 1925-6, was even more intense. This time international Bolshevism, inspired and organized by Russian agitators, stirred the colony into an ideological frenzy which was to reduce the city to its knees.

This time the war lasted for six months. The students of the elite colonial educational establishment, Queen's College, were chosen by the agitators in Hong Kong to fulfil their historic role in China—to lead the masses to victory over the colonial and capitalist enemy, the foreign businessmen and government officials in the concessions, and in Hong Kong itself.

The chief centres of this eruption were, of course, the major Chinese cities—Shanghai, Beijing, Tianjin and Guangzhou. Guangzhou experienced a bloody civil war, its insurrectionaries claiming to be the national government of China.[8] Again events in Guangzhou overflowed into Hong Kong and a Hong Kong Labour Commission emerged from its Hoi Yuen chrysalis to put an ultimatum to the government. Six demands were made, including an eight-hour working day, the right for Chinese to reside on the Peak, and Chinese representation by popular ballot on the Legislative Council. Failing acceptance of their demands, the Hong Kong Chinese would again march to Guangzhou.

Then in June, Chinese demonstrators fired upon the foreign settlement on Shameen (Shamian) Island in Guangzhou. It appeared, as Austin Coates suggests, that 'the integrity of the community was about to be put to the test'. Coates recounts an inspiring tale of patriotic Europeans. The Hong Kong Hotel ran an emergency bus service, and J A Taggart, the general manager, and his wife personally served the guests. In this confrontation of the races, too, there were a few 'loyal' (to Hong Kong and Britain) local Chinese workers who were zealous in their voluntary services and kept the city running.

But this time, even more so than in 1922, there was greater economic and social paralysis, as well as the constant threat of terror. The weapons of rumour, intimidation and withholding of labour wielded by the strikers were now reinforced by economic warfare—runs on the banks and embargoes. The port came to a standstill. Eventually when the 16-month strike was over the British government in London had to make a £30-million loan to the business community to get it on its feet again.

The defeat of Chinese nationalism in alliance with international communism in 1926 did not remove either

Stamps issued to commemorate the centenary celebrations of Hong Kong (1841-1941) (above); the Peninsula Hotel, pre-World War II (below)

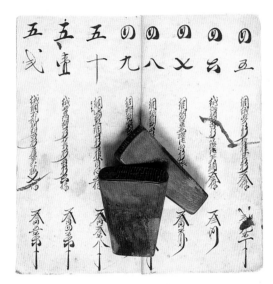

A Cheung Chau pawn broker's chop, early twentieth century

influence from Hong Kong. To the republican revolutionaries, Hong Kong, because of its proximity to the stage of action and to sources of funds and arms, was a bridgehead for subversion, despite official discouragement. Even during the crises of the 1920s, Russian agents operating in China had free access to Hong Kong.

Four years later, another of the great Asian revolutionaries, Ho Chi Minh, was active in the colony organizing the secret Indo-China Communist Party on behalf of the Comintern.

Under the alias Nguyen Ai Quoc, Ho Chi Minh and his girlfriend Li Sam were arrested and detained without warrant in June 1931 at an address near Kowloon City. The French Sûreté had tracked them here from French Indo-China. The Hong Kong Government was anxious to obtain an extradition order for the pair.

The official policy, clear in principle but difficult to carry out, was to grant asylum to political refugees (as it had done earlier to the rebel Philippine nationalists, Aguinaldo and Rizal), but not to condone the use of the territory as a base for fomenting trouble in neighbouring countries. Ho and his lawyers, however, were able to exploit ambiguities in this approach and succeeded in forcing the Hong Kong Government to accommodate him in considerable comfort in the Bowen Road Military Hospital on the Peak for over 18 months. Moreover, when the case went up to the Privy Council in London, where Ho was represented by Sir Stafford Cripps Q C, the Hong Kong Government was 'squeezed' into paying Ho's legal expenses. They also arranged for his departure to Shanghai, where he would be safe from his secret-police enemies, who were anxious to carry out the death penalty ordered by the Vietnamese courts. Ho left Hong Kong in the middle of the night on Chinese New Year's Eve—26 January 1933— and was smuggled on board a ship in the Lei Yue Mun Channel, the eastern entrance of Hong Kong harbour. Hong Kong's governor, Sir William Peel, had the chagrin of realizing not only that the Government had been obliged to assist Ho in 'getting back in touch with the Russian principals', but also of failing to be reimbursed for the expense of Ho's stay in Hong Kong by the French Government!

Ho Chi Minh's presence in the territory was not a direct threat to Hong Kong. The looming threat, which eventually was to overtake the colony, was at that time being exhibited in northern China, in Manchuria. The year 1931 saw the Mukden Incident, which was the first stage in the systematic build-up of aggression by the forces of Japanese imperialism. This incident and the notorious Marco Polo Bridge episode near Beijing in 1937 were military demonstrations to force Republican China to accept Japanese hegemony. But in the course of this explosion of Japanese nationalism, the Treaty Ports and the international settlement at Shanghai were also subjected to both blatant and subtle forms of pressure and intimidation. The Chinese Maritime Customs came under the control of Japanese officialdom, a circumstance which affected Hong Kong's commercial and financial links with the China coast.

The 1930s were, in fact, also a period of deep crisis for the struggling colonial economy. The colony's traders, bankers and few industrialists had been severely hit by the worldwide depression. This was the nadir of business prosperity. Despite attempts by both London and the local administration to find new industries and to boost tourism (to be based at the newly-opened Peninsula and Repulse Bay hotels), trade was in the doldrums.

In 1937, Japan opened up its 'Special Undeclared War' against Chiang Kai-shek. Its naval and aerial blockade of the Pearl River Estuary was like a noose around the colony's main entry point to southern China—Guangzhou itself was invaded by Japanese troops in October 1938. The Kowloon—Canton Railway was also bombed and shipping was fired upon, vessels seized and even neutral Hong Kong-British planes and ships were subject to harassment by the aggressors.

In this prelude to the invasion of Hong Kong, the colony celebrated its centenary as a British territory of the empire. The celebrations were low-key. Hong Kong was supposedly in the hands of 'a man of iron', Lieutenant General E F Norton, the acting governor and commander-in-chief of the forces, and Hong Kong had to be disciplined to offer 'stern resistance' to the Japanese threat.

But it was as much Chinese sensitivity to the Hong Kong issue, even though in these pre-war years Chiang Kai-shek had offered to negotiate an extended lease of the New Territories in exchange for a loan, which prompted *The Times* to observe, 'A proper regard for Chinese susceptibilities, which have been rendered particularly acute because of the Japanese aggression, has prevented the British authorities in Hong Kong from celebrating the centenary of its cession to Britain.' The mood was sombre, even though the military reassured the civil population that the worst would not happen. But there were other shadows, too.

The Hon. Man Kam Lo, a senior Legislative Council member who had investigated the hawking and squatting problems of the city now swollen with refugees, asked a number of questions, some of which remain unanswered today. 'Can we be content', he addressed his celebrated audience, 'with the prevalence of squalor and abject poverty of the masses, the existence of slums; the lack, or inadequacy, of social services such as hospitals, sanitariums, workmen's compensation and industrial insurance . . . ?' Perhaps Hong Kong was on the way to becoming a proper model of Western and Chinese cooperation creating a decent and flourishing city on the China coast, where its citizens might enjoy a greater degree of dignity and prosperity than in China itself. After all, the 1930s had seen moves by the government to investigate housing conditions, even to institute a minimum wage for its workers, and the colony's medical services were also being updated by the energetic Sir Selwyn-Clarke, the director of medical services.

It was Sir Robert Hotung (1862-1956), a Jardine comprador and businessman in his own right, who epitomized the Hong Kong success story, and who, almost a centenarian himself, expressed Hong Kong's true genius. Although he would not be alive to enjoy the celebrations of Hong Kong's bicentenary in the year 2041, he had every confidence that Hong Kong would, and that it would be 'a fair city'. Much took place in the years following the centenary of British occupation to dim that optimism.

1

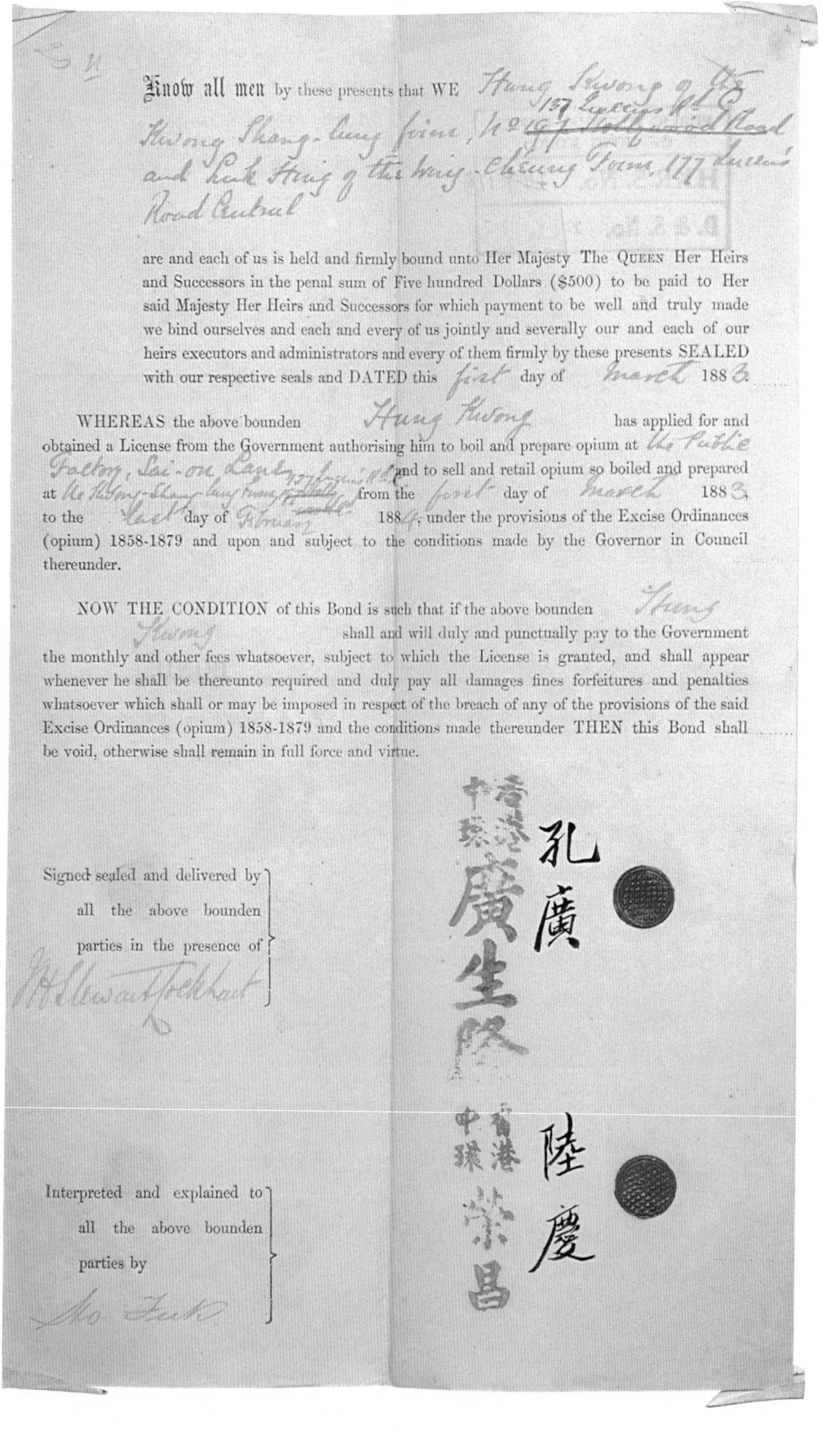

Know all men by these presents that WE *Hung Kwong of the*
157 Queen's Rd C
Kwong Shang-lung firm, No 167 Hollywood Road
and Luk Hing of the Wing-Cheung Firm, 177 Queen's
Road Central

are and each of us is held and firmly bound unto Her Majesty The QUEEN Her Heirs
and Successors in the penal sum of Five hundred Dollars ($500) to be paid to Her
said Majesty Her Heirs and Successors for which payment to be well and truly made
we bind ourselves and each and every of us jointly and severally our and each of our
heirs executors and administrators and every of them firmly by these presents SEALED
with our respective seals and DATED this *first* day of *March* 188*3*

WHEREAS the above bounden *Hung Kwong* has applied for and
obtained a License from the Government authorising him to boil and prepare opium at *the Public*
Factory, Sai-on Lan by Queen's No and to sell and retail opium so boiled and prepared
at *the Kwong-Shang-lung Firm, specially* from the *first* day of *March* 188*3*,
to the *last* day of *February* 188*4*, under the provisions of the Excise Ordinances
(opium) 1858-1879 and upon and subject to the conditions made by the Governor in Council
thereunder.

NOW THE CONDITION of this Bond is such that if the above bounden *Hung*
Kwong shall and will duly and punctually pay to the Government
the monthly and other fees whatsoever, subject to which the License is granted, and shall appear
whenever he shall be thereunto required and duly pay all damages fines forfeitures and penalties
whatsoever which shall or may be imposed in respect of the breach of any of the provisions of the said
Excise Ordinances (opium) 1858-1879 and the conditions made thereunder THEN this Bond shall
be void, otherwise shall remain in full force and virtue.

Signed sealed and delivered by 〕
all the above bounden 〕
parties in the presence of 〕
H Stewart Lockhart

香港
中環
廣生號

孔廣
生號

Interpreted and explained to 〕
all the above bounden 〕
parties by 〕
Ko Fuk

香港
中環
榮昌

陸慶
榮昌

3

4

5

6

7

8

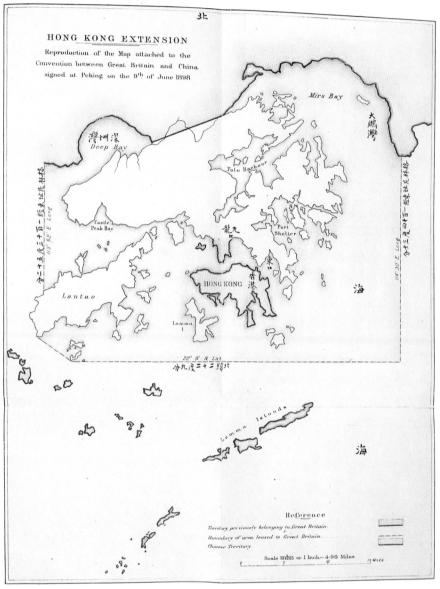

9

10

11

12

13

14

15

16

17

18

19

20

21

22

23

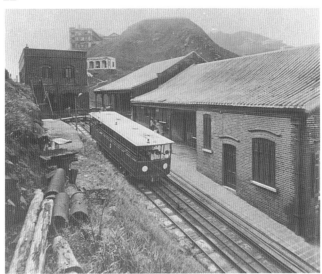

24

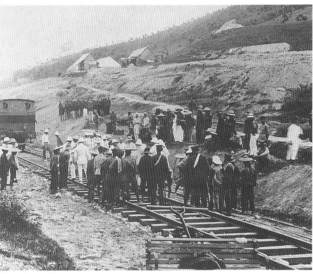

25

26

27

Hongkong, Resting Place of the highest spot of the Peak.

28

HONGKONG AND SHANGHAI BANK BUILDING, HONGKONG.

29

Captions (pages 42-54)

1   *View of Hong Kong harbour and Victoria Peak 1862, unknown Chinese artist*

2   *Licence to 'boil and prepare' opium issued to Hung Kwong by the Hong Kong Government, March 1883*

3   *Governor Sir John Pope Hennessy (1877-1882)*

4   *Governor Sir William Des Voeux (1887-1891)*

5   *Governor Sir Henry Pottinger (1843-1844), Hong Kong's first governor*

6   *Governor Sir Arthur Kennedy (1872-1877)*

7   *Governor Sir William Robinson (1891-1898) with members of the Legislative Council, 1897*

8   *Governor Sir Frederick Lugard (1907-1920), with Chinese guests at Government House, 1907*

9   *Map accompanying the 1898 Convention of Peking demarcating the area (New Territories) to be leased to Britain by China*

10   *The Botanical Gardens were established by Governor Sir John Bowring in the 1860s, with the aim of bringing together a wide variety of Chinese plants and trees*

11   *The Peak, 1905, taken from an album presented to Jardine, Matheson and Company Ltd.*

12   *A Chinese baker, E Sing, conspired to poison the European population of Victoria by putting arsenic in his bread, apparently on the orders of mandarins in Canton,* Illustrated London News, *28 March, 1857*

13   *How Qua (Wu Ping Ch'ien), (1769-1843), the chief of the association of senior merchants, known as the Co-Hong, in Canton, by George Chinnery, c 1830*

14   *Sir Boshan Wei Yuk (1849-1921), Comprador of the Chartered Mercantile Bank, Justice of the Peace (1883), an unofficial member of the Legislative Council representing the Chinese community and member of the Sanitary Board*

15   *Sir James Stewart Lockhart and Dr Ho Kai assembled with members of the Tung Wah Hospital Group for the opening of the Po Leung Kuk, 1896*

16   *'Soldiers of the Shropshire Regiment burning wooden partitions removed from infected houses,'* Illustrated London News, *28 July, 1894*

17   *'West Point, Hong-Kong (densely populated), where the plague first appeared,'* Illustrated London News, *30 June, 1894*

18   *A 1930s Chinese bazaar in Bonham Strand, Hong Kong Island*

19   *Happy Valley race course c 1881*

20   *Hong Kong society at the races, early 1900s*

21   *The fire at Happy Valley which claimed hundreds of lives, 1918*

22   *Tiger shot in the New Territories after killing two police officers, 1915*

23   *Typhoon along the waterfront 1906*

24   *The Peak Tramway from the Cathedral to Victoria Gap, opened in 1888*

25   *The British section of the Kowloon—Canton Railway was completed in 1910*

26   *Taikoo sugar refinery in its heyday, operated by Butterfield and Swire, was Hong Kong's largest industrial enterprise*

27   *In the early 1900s the Hong Kong Club formed the heart of the colony's business and social life*

28/29   *Postcards from the early 1900s showing the highest point on the Peak and the Hongkong and Shanghai Bank building*

THE PORT OF HONG KONG

The harbour of Hong Kong Island can be approached through the narrow Lei Yue Mun Channel to the east and the Lamma and Kap Shui Mun channels to the west. In its myriad of bays it has always afforded temporary shelter to ships which, before Britain took possession and developed the area, could get essential supplies, particularly water, from the waterfalls plunging down the rocky outcrops of this island as well as outlying islands.

Urmston Road, just west of Tuen Mun, once said to be in Portuguese possession, is today projected as the new port of Hong Kong. Nearby is the island of Lintin, once the offshore base for the opium trade. This area was an important anchorage for the merchant sailing ships of the European trading companies which had their headquarters in Guangzhou and their summer retreats in the Portuguese enclave of Macau. In the eighteenth century this section of the Pearl River—between Macau and Guangzhou—was the only area of Chinese soil on which the Chinese emperor would permit foreigners to trade.

It was the inconveniences and irritations

of the limiting Canton System of trade which drove the British to make Hong Kong Island a non-Chinese territory. After the conquests of the First Opium War of 1839-42, a permanent trading depot was established there.

In the nineteenth century Hong Kong grew to be the port handling the third largest turnover of tonnage in the British Empire. Then, as now, Hong Kong was home-port for a considerable fleet of sailing ships, steamships and ocean-liners. It was also home to a motley collection of tramp steamers plying between the China coastal ports and the inland treaty ports. Passenger ferries sailed mostly between Hong Kong, Shanghai and Guangzhou. And, of course, there was the large flock of attendant native craft—the junks, sampans and lorchas expertly steered by the local maritime population.

There were four major steamship companies controlling the seas in the nineteenth century: the China Navigation Company, the China Merchants' Steamship Company, the China Coast Steam Navigation Company and the Indo-China Steamship Company Limited. Together they operated some 100 vessels of approximately 100,000 tons in total.

Today Hong Kong company-operated ships are registered in overseas ports and are part of a worldwide network of shipping lines and ship charterers. These include bulk carriers of oil, ores and other basic commodities. But prior to World War II, the Hong Kong shipping connection was mainly based on the China

coast and in Southeast Asia.

Yet Hong Kong was also an important port of call for international passenger steamships. In the halcyon days of travel by liner, Hong Kong's harbour and wharves were graced by ships from America, Canada, France, Holland and Japan as well as the descendants of pioneering British steamship lines such as the illustrious Peninsular and Oriental Line. As early as 1844, the Lady Mary Wood had inaugurated the famous P & O route to the Far East.

The advent of the multiple-engine steamship, the major technological innovation in international transport in the nineteenth century, has almost obliterated the memory of the romantic sailing ship. But for a brief period during the gold-crazed decade of the 1840s, Hong Kong was a temporary home for the American whaling fleet which sought its prey in the icy waters of the southern Pacific Ocean.

Vital to Hong Kong's success was its position as the second most important port of loading for the China tea trade. Tea, which symbolizes the China trade even more than silk or opium, was conducted out of Hong Kong from 1848 to 1876. In the sailing season of 1869-70 this trade reached its zenith, with as many as nine tea clippers tied up alongside the Hong Kong wharves. Names like Black Prince, Lothair, Lochinvar, Invincible and Sea Witch live on in the roll call of that era's most graceful and fastest sailing ships.

The China trade has always been important to Hong Kong. At the end of the nineteenth century the port's ships carried between 20 and 30 percent of China's imports and exports. For example, in the 1920s over 40 million tons entered the port. But following the maritime strikes and boycott of 1925-26, the China trade collapsed dramatically, demonstrating the

Butterfield and Swire ship anchored in Hong Kong harbour at the time of the Russo-Japanese war, 1905 (preceding page); Canadian passenger liner, Tsim Sha Tsui, 1930s (above)

dependence on China for the port's prosperity. Two important factors in the growth of the port were the opening of the Suez Canal (1869) and the Panama Canal (1914).

The river and ocean trade was unloaded by lighters and sampans which transferred the cargoes from the holds of the ships anchored midstream to godowns on the shore. This efficient method still continues despite the superior bulk services of Hong Kong's eight container terminals. These terminals, built over the last 20 years, help make Hong Kong the busiest container port in the world.

Warehouses were among the first buildings to appear on Hong Kong Island in the 1840s. As reclamation and the annexation of the Kowloon Peninsula provided more land at the water's edge, wharves and dockyards were built. Hung Hom is one of the areas that was created in this way.

With the development of the Kowloon side, the balance of trading activity shifted from Hong Kong across the harbour. But Hong Kong remained a more convenient disembarking point for the luxury liners and Royal Navy warships. Today the only major dockyard on the island is HMS Tamar, until World War II the headquarters of the China Station. Now there are plans to transfer that facility to Stonecutters Island in the harbour near Kowloon. If this move goes ahead, the Royal Dockyard, for years a major impediment to Hong Kong Island's development, will be reclaimed and become the site for yet more commercial towers.

The last merchant sailing ships were put into port just before World War II. Now, the only reminders of those days are the occasional courtesy calls paid by barquentine-brigs used as training ships.

The river steamships and ferries have given way to motorized junks and hydrofoils which speed along between Hong Kong and the ports in the Pearl River estuary. Macau, with its gambling casinos and quaint sights is a particularly powerful magnet for both Hong Kong gamblers and tourists who come to experience the East.

Hong Kong is still a busy base for fishing fleets which now trawl the South China Sea in concrete-hulled boats. The chief fishing ports in Hong Kong are Aberdeen, Shau Kei Wan and Sham Shui Po.

The unprecedented industrial growth of the colony and the expansion of the international market has relieved to some extent its dependence on the China trade. Hong Kong port still enjoys growing prosperity. It now handles 80 million tons of cargo a year, an increase of almost 90 percent over the past five years.

There is a well-founded expectation that with closer links to China, now embarked precariously on its modernization programme, the port of Hong Kong must expand its own marine facilities. Plans for the construction of a second major port in Hong Kong's western waters, and a new airport to serve both Hong Kong and southern China have now been concluded.

The future will inevitably bring changes, but Hong Kong's traditional dependence on the sea as a highway and to a lesser extent as an important food source will not change.

Kwai Chung is currently the busiest container terminal in the world

PART TWO

The Rising Sun

Hong Kong During the
Japanese Occupation
1 9 4 1 - 4 5

There is nothing to stop Japan from seizing French Indo-China, the
Netherlands Indies or Hong Kong . . .

Report of the Japanese director of military intelligence, June 1940.

The battle for Hong Kong was a brief affair. Unlike the Japanese-Malayan campaign, culminating in the fall of Singapore—chief bastion of the British Empire in the East—there was never really any question about the conclusion.

The battle for Hong Kong was fought in two acts—from 8 to 12 December 1941 for the New Territories and the Kowloon Peninsula, and from 18 December to Christmas Day for the island proper. There was considerable bloodshed on both sides. Militarily, Hong Kong was indefensible, particularly because it lacked adequate air power to neutralize invading forces. The entire Royal Air Force detachment at Kai Tak Airport consisted of less than ten sluggish, outmoded amphibious planes. The airport was put out of action in the first Japanese air raid at 7 am on 8 December, signalling the beginning of the march on Hong Kong.

A more decisive factor in the British defeat was psychology. Firstly, the city's population had recently grown because of the addition of more than a million Chinese refugees from across the border, who represented no more than a temporary impediment for the combatants. When the guns fell silent, many of them would be raped, trussed together with cord or wire and dumped into the harbour. The more fortunate enjoyed a reprieve before being put into unseaworthy junks, supposedly for repatriation to China, but they soon disappeared at sea. The population was reduced by more than a million people, some of whom, tossed about by the tides of war, fled back to their homeland in southern China, where the Japanese had carried out scorched earth campaigns. But it is a safe estimate that at least half of those expelled from the island fortress of Hong Kong perished in watery graves in the South China Sea.

But what of the small core of Chinese Hong Kong residents who had either been born in the colony or who had carried on business here and were well established in the local community? What of the people who were prominent, for instance, in the Tung Wah Hospital directorate or the Watchmen's Committee, or even in the long-established district Kaifong (neighbourhood) Associations? Many of them had been educated in the top local schools and at Hong Kong University. They had ties of class and education, and had become a potentially loyal body of citizen soldiers, ready to fight for their 'homeland'.

The inevitable scandals surrounding a less-than-efficient colonial administration desperately trying to organize Hong Kong upon a war footing—corruption over air-raid shelters and blackout materials, for example—did not greatly offend the local business community. But badly conceived and fumbling policies of racial discrimination did. The question of nationality was an emotive one. Such was the case over the evacuation of dependents of British residents before the hostilities began. In many cases, wives wanted to stay; some women who went to the Philippines in 1940 returned surreptitiously; husbands separated from their families also clamoured for their return. There was division among the European ranks, between those who had 'pull' and could get around the restrictions, and those who could not.

Flag showing a message from a Japanese
commander to a subordinate officer during
the battle for Hong Kong, 8-25 December, 1941
(above); Victoria Cross awarded to Sergeant-
Major Osborne, the only VC ever to be
awarded in Hong Kong (below)

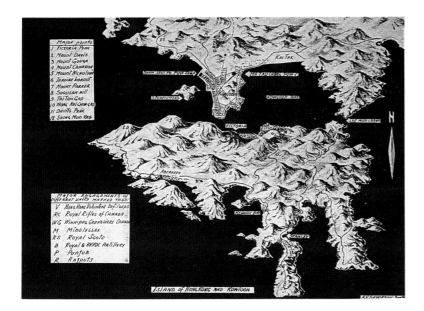

Map of the British defence positions on Hong Kong Island and Kowloon, December 1941 (left); woodblock, by a Chinese artist, of Kowloon wharf, January 1942 (right)

There were no British Dependent Territories passports then, but discrimination prevailed against Chinese holders of British passports who claimed the privilege of evacuation for their wives. According to the local interpretation of the Emergency Regulations, these Britons did not qualify. The inevitable result was much bitterness and resentment against the *gweilo* (foreign) population. Only the rapid escalation of events prevented this issue from becoming a festering sore of alienation.

The British commanders, however, did not believe that the local population could be relied upon if hostilities broke out—the xenophobia of the organized crime syndicates, known as the triads, probably fostered this unhappy conviction. Somewhat reluctantly, they allowed local Portuguese men who had worked for institutions like the government and the banks to enlist in special companies of volunteers; but they stood fast against recruiting Chinese companies. Local men could be conscripted to drive lorries and for other service jobs, but they were not entrusted with firearms to defend themselves and their families. Even the Royal Hong Kong Police had no Chinese NCOs, or inspectors of officer rank.

The result was that a golden opportunity to give a significant section of the community a chance to express its loyalty to Hong Kong, and even to Britain, was lost. A local university doctor and part-time soldier, Sir Lindsay Ride, escaped from Hong Kong upon the British surrender on Christmas Day, 1941, just 18 days after the 'special undeclared war' had been declared. In his view Hong Kong fell even before the battle had begun. There was a disastrous disaffection of the population which, given the conditions of the time, could not have been expected to be loyal *en masse* to the local government.

As the battle raged, detachments of Japanese troops infiltrated through and over the hills, mopping up the scattered and uncoordinated pockets of British, Indian and Canadian resistance. There were rumours of 'fifth columnists' leaving markers and tracks for the enemy. On the hillsides in the New Territories, one can still find permanent signs leading to British outposts and to the headquarters of the Royal Scots, the Rajputs and the Punjabi regiments, the defenders of

Japanese troops marching through the streets of Kowloon, 28 December, 1941

the Gin-drinkers line. Possibly some local Chinese were coerced into assisting the enemy. But there was an enemy within which had to be dealt with, either by being eliminated or bought off.

A Chinese officer stationed in Hong Kong, Admiral Chan Chak, was in charge of a force and given a free hand to eliminate fifth columnists. He claimed to have trapped and killed several hundred Japanese sympathizers in a Western District cinema. Despite this, protection rackets grew, most probably run by triad members taking advantage of the dislocation of all supplies. According to a former member of the Criminal Investigation Department of the Royal Hong Kong Police, a series of secret deals were set up to persuade the triads not to carry out their planned threat of killing off all the Europeans in Hong Kong. Apparently a deal was struck whereby IOUs totalling several million dollars were issued to be paid at the end of the war—with the Allies' victory. It is not known whether this part of the bargain was ever kept.

The battle itself was a reluctant affair. Indeed, General Maltby,[9] the commander of Hong Kong's armed forces, in his later account and apologia for the British failure of arms, claimed in extenuation that his troops were 'hostages to fortune'. The resistance was, after all, a forlorn gesture to redeem Winston Churchill's pledge that the British Empire would not easily be surrendered. The governor at the time, Sir Mark Young, also agonized about giving in to the two Japanese ultimata, issued in the interval of the Hong Kong battle, to spare the city the ravages of the inevitable destruction resulting from the fighting.

Nevertheless, local veterans like the famous Hughesliers, commanded by the Jardine taipan The Honourable J J Paterson, put up a stern resistance to hold the North Point Power Station on Hong Kong Island. Maintaining vital utilities to keep the garrison and civil population going was critical, and once the Japanese 228th Regiment had secured the chief source of water, the recently-opened Shing Mun (Jubilee) Reservoir in the New Territories, it was only a matter of time before an unconditional surrender would follow. The 50-year-old veterans of the volunteer force stood directly in the path of the three-pronged attack across the harbour, designed to sweep up to the commanding heights above the city and then wheel around to drive Victoria's defenders into the sea again.

Great tenacity was shown during the last stages of the battle by the remnants of the regular regiments, who were supposed to group together to prevent the invaders from cutting a fatal swathe right across the island.

Above the strategic Wong Nei Chung Gap in the middle of the island there was a police station, which commanded the roads up from Causeway Bay, Happy Valley, Deepwater Bay and Stanley. When its ammunition had been spent, rocks and boulders were hurled from the station down the hillside to halt, temporarily, the indefatigable march of infantrymen .

Canadian Sergeant-Major, RM Osborne, won his Victoria Cross in December 1941 on a height overlooking the site of the current-day Cricket Club. By then there were isolated but ferocious skirmishes. Osborne flung himself upon an enemy grenade and won a permanent place in Hong Kong's military history. This battle was an affair of the regiments—the Middlesex and Royal Scots, in particular.

Further down the road on the seashore there was another epic struggle. The beautiful Repulse Bay Hotel, once a 'Riviera' retreat for Hong Kong high society, was now a haven for the army and navy, and a gallant band of civilians. This band had a military commander, but its true leader was a nurse, Miss Mosey. For three days while the hotel was under siege, the civilians sheltered in a storm-water tunnel running under the hotel down to the beach. Eventually, the hundred or so soldiers also escaped by this subterranean passage to make a last stand at Stanley.

Once this battle was over for the hotel guests they were faced with another ordeal. At nearby Eucliffe, the gothic-castellated mansion of Eu Tong-sen, the Southeast-Asian millionaire, these reluctant guests of the Imperial Army were treated to another bloody spectacle. The battle-fevered troops of Colonel Tanaka held a mass execution of captured British soldiers. Lined up on the wall, facing the swimming pool, with their backs to the sea, they were systematically bayonetted and thrown down on the rocks below to be swept away by the currents of the South China Sea.

Yet another atrocity occurred at Stanley where the battle was in its last throes. Ironically, this southern peninsula of the island was the best defended, with large guns and a concentration of troops. But, as in Singapore, the military planners had apparently been expecting an attack from the sea and the guns were also 'facing the wrong way'.

With or without artillery support, the defenders of this garrison fought to the death at the hands of an implacable enemy. At 4 am on Christmas Day, just when war-weary General Maltby was trying to plan an honourable surrender, sending urgent despatches to the governor, Sir Mark Young (who reportedly was consoling himself by playing Beethoven on his gramophone in Government House), a small group of Tanaka's troops swept into St Stephens College. It housed a temporary field hospital under a Red Cross flag. In a savage burst of blood-lust, the patients were bayonetted in their beds and the nurses raped and killed.

The fighting lingered on until the official cease-fire. The governor and the armed forces' commander were ferried across the harbour to the Peninsula Hotel in Kowloon, now serving

The signing of the British surrender by Governor Sir Mark Young, 25 December, 1941 at the Peninsula Hotel

as the headquarters of the Japanese commander, Lieutenant-General Takashi Sakai. The British surrendered at 3 pm in a room dimly lit by a row of candles. News of this climax of the battle for Hong Kong was not easily communicated to the distant defenders of the British Empire. The end of the first imperial century for the British was marked by a messy affair. The flag torn down at Stanley was made of the tattered, bloodstained shreds of hospital sheeting from the military hospital where another massacre had taken place.

This conquest of Hong Kong was a mere sideshow compared with the major Japanese offensives at Pearl Harbor, the Philippines and the Malay Peninsula. In strict strategic terms it could be argued that the campaign was not needed by the Japanese. Any supportive role that Hong Kong might have played in the battles in Southeast Asia was neutralized in December 1941 by the sinking of the battleships *Repulse* and *Prince of Wales*.

The Chinese theatre of war was under the command of Chiang Kai-shek. (Late in the war the Americans had planned a seaborne invasion of southern China, with Hong Kong as its beachhead, but this operation never left the drawing board.) During the brief interval of action in the New Territories, and indeed even before the outbreak of hostilities, Chiang had spread rumours that a relieving force from Changsha was on its way to liberate the beleaguered garrison. But the first offers were spurned by the British and the relieving force never materialized.

The Japanese had included the Western-occupied territories of China and Southeast Asia on their map of *The Greater East Asia Co-Prosperity Sphere*. The oppressed peoples of Asia were supposed to be liberated by their fellow Asian warriors. But if the Japanese encouraged independence movements in the Philippines, Indonesia and elsewhere, Hong Kong was not important enough to merit such treatment. Hong Kong was promulgated as an 'Occupied Territory'. It seems from the present-day ruins of a few fortified positions that the Japanese gave the island some small credit as a strategic site, possibly to defend the approaches to the Pearl River and Guangzhou. The only positive role for the former British dependency to play was as a very small base for the manufacture of some essential equipment required for the Pacific war effort.

Hong Kong, then, was not a great asset, and the Japanese did not intend for it to become a liability. Even just to maintain Hong Kong at its pre-war level of existence would have been an unwarranted luxury. The wealth was drained off both directly and indirectly. The Chinese merchants and industrialists were 'voluntarily' organized into associations to aid the Japanese fighting machine. In reality, they would be subjected to the time-honoured process of the squeeze.

The Japanese began by drawing up a comprehensive inventory of the buildings they occupied—the hotels, stores, clubs (the Hong Kong Club became the Naval Officers' Club) and churches (the cathedral was then serving as livery stables). Government House was rendered nearly uninhabitable as a result of tunnelling underneath to create a hiding place for some of the fabulous Chater Collection of art treasures, to date still unrecovered. The first Japanese governor, General Rensuke Isogai, chose not to live there, settling for a more pleasant location on the Repulse Bay Road. This was close to the Repulse Bay Hotel,

The Japanese Governor of Hong Kong, Lieutenant-General Rensuke Isogai, with prominent local citizens, 1942 (above); coaster used at the 'Toa' Hotel (Peninsula Hotel), Tsim Sha Tsui, during the Japanese Occupation (below)

Currency issued by the Japanese occupying forces in Hong Kong

itself to be refurbished as the Midoyama Hotel, a rest centre for Japanese troops. The official governor's residence in Central, the basis of which survives to the present day, was reconstructed by the Japanese only much later, in 1943.

The rest of the victor's bureaucratic plans took shape in the occupied Hongkong and Shanghai Bank premises; but the task of listing every desk, chair and typewriter proved to be too vast and the inventory of spoils was never properly carried out.

As is well known, the Japanese had a rigorous attitude to hygiene. The uncounted civilian fatalities of the war constituted a health hazard, and it was necessary to organize a clean-up. (Later, when starvation took a hold, corpses did not stay in the gutter for long; there was cannibalism in Hong Kong and human flesh could be bought in the street markets.) The survivors, whether they were prisoners of war in the Kowloon camps, European civilians confined to Stanley Internment Camp, or the local Chinese, were all constantly tested for infection and given injections.

Some attempts were made, too, by Japanese officials to grow enough food for the reduced population by enrolling local experts such as former administrative officer Kennedy-Skipton, to advise farmers in the use of night soil. It is not known how successful the agricultural experiments in the New Territories were. However, as the war continued, zealous officials were replaced by less inspired ones, and attempts to run Hong Kong efficiently were abandoned. Finally, one Japanese governor is reputed to have shrugged his shoulders and said, 'Let them eat grass!' There was plenty of it growing in the middle of the empty streets.

Everything was run down. It was impossible to stay in Hong Kong without proper documentation; and such documentation was only issued to those with a proper job. And as office and factory equipment was either shipped off to Japan, or fell into disuse, there were fewer and fewer jobs. Indeed many were faced with a diminishing set of options: a march northwards across the Chinese border, or a one-way boat ticket to Macau.

The Japanese occupying authorities froze bank accounts which were then gradually evaporated by exchanging Hong Kong dollars for devalued Japanese military yen. Hong Kong's business elite, the bankers, were kept in former brothels along the Western waterfront and marched every day to the counting houses to balance the books and to sign 'duress' currency. These banknotes were honoured by

Sketch from a Chinese magazine published in 1943, depicting daily life in Hong Kong during the Occupation (above); sketch drawn by prisoner of war, Lieutenant Skorzvov, in Sham Shui Po camp (middle); sketch drawn by a civilian internee at Stanley camp (below)

the Hongkong and Shanghai Bank after the war, although, in an attempt to protect the bank's liquidity, there had been a gigantic bonfire of banknotes on the Peak during the last days of the battle to prevent them from falling into enemy hands.

Attempts were made to 'Japanize' the names of Hong Kong's prominent buildings and streets. Queen's Road became Nakameiji-dori; Des Voeux Road became Katorido-dori. The Gloucester Hotel was renamed the Matsubara; and the Peninsula, the most important, the Toa (Great Eastern).

A few schools continued to operate and were obliged to include the Japanese language in their syllabuses; but the Catholic teaching fathers were often arrested and confined in Stanley Prison (next to the civilian internment camp) on charges of espionage. The university did not function as a teaching establishment during the war. Its library was integrated with a few other book collections from the Helena May Institute. Some rare items found their way to the Toyo Bunko library in Tokyo, but were retrieved after the war. The number of students in the colony dwindled to a mere 2,500 by the end of the war.

The impression which the Japanese occupying forces made upon the local population was one of erratic terror. One of the most noticeable measures introduced by the conquerors was the midday 'freeze': when important Japanese officers were being driven to work, everyone on the street had to stand motionless until the cavalcade had passed. There were a few cases of conspiratorial connivance between individuals and officials who bent the rules for mutual benefit.

Hong Kong's indifference towards its overlords gave the Japanese authorities little scope to sponsor local candidates in an independence movement directed against the former British colonialists. There were a number of citizens of Indian descent who were viewed as an anomalous body with disputed imperial ties of citizenship, but Japanese attempts to associate local Indian policeman, in particular, with the fifth-column Indian Nationalist Army were neither whole-hearted nor successful. There were also individual bankers, stock-brokers and hoteliers who were nationals of neutral countries and classified by the Japanese as 'third nationals'. Occasionally Britons, in order to escape the rigours of confinement, masqueraded as Irish citizens and were thus allowed a certain freedom of movement in Hong Kong.

In the Kowloon prisoner-of-war camps at Sham Shui Po and Argyle Street, there were deeper animosities and clearer allegiances. The few thousand Allied troops who were caged behind barbed-wire were in constant fear of being drafted to work in locomotive workshops or coalmines in Japan; they would endure hunger, hardship and alienation from the local population and also risked being bombed by the American Air Force planes flying from bases in China, creating havoc and destruction among the Japanese cities.

As the grip of the Allies on the lifelines of the new Japanese empire tightened, with their submarines controlling the sea lanes to Japan, there was a growing risk that these slave-labourers would be sent to the bottom of the sea by their own navy. This, in fact, happened a number of times, the most notorious case being that of the *Lisbon Maru* in 1942. Its battened-down holds were full of Royal Scots and Middlesex Regiment prisoners of war from Sham Shui Po, when it was torpedoed by an American submarine. In all several hundred were

毋忘五月八日廣州市，美機濫炸無辜平民事件

市民諸君！

防空準備妥當了嗎？

積極準備空防，避免無謂犧牲！

香港占領地總督部

Propaganda poster issued during the Second World War by the Japanese authorities, aimed at the local civilian population

drowned; the rest somehow managed to clamber ashore on a remote island off the Chinese coast. But there was no salvation for them either. Their Chinese rescuers could not keep them out of the hands of the Japanese masters and the survivors were eventually shipped to Japan again.

Hong Kong was a prison for the British and other Europeans during the war, if only because of its physical isolation. Few military prisoners could risk a journey to the Mainland; with no common language they would have no means of crossing an alien land to the Kuomintang (Nationalist) war-time capital at Chongqing (Chungking).

Of course, a few intrepid individuals escaped successfully, thanks to both planning and luck. The thousands of remaining troops and dock workers needed an escape line, with escorts and safe-houses. This was provided by the impromptu and informal British Army Aid Group (BAAG) established in March 1942. BAAG was founded by the redoubtable Colonel Lindsay Ride, a former Hong Kong University

Japanese soldier surrenders to British forces,
August 1945

professor of medicine, who simply walked out of the camp with a couple of colleagues in the days before the gates of the prison were bolted tight. Ride and his university colleagues escaped to Waichow and then, after a remarkably quick evacuation to Chongqing, won the patronage of Madame Chiang, the Generalissimo's wife.

Starting life as a modest escape-and-evasion affair, BAAG grew into an informal army, establishing forward posts in the New Territories. One of its lieutenants, Ronnie Holmes, later Hong Kong's colonial secretary, led a band of guerrillas that blew up tunnels on the Kowloon—Canton Railway, made reconnoitres of Kai Tak Airport, and even stuck patriotic posters on the doors of Central Market. Knowledge of such actions boosted the morale of the Britons inside the camps. The organization also succeeded in smuggling out large numbers of workers who found their way to the naval base of Colombo in Ceylon.

Ride, in every sense a 'big' man, wanted to liberate Hong Kong himself, if only because he thought that the British colonialists had disappointed the Hong Kong people and their allies on the Mainland. An Australian by birth and a latter-day Morrison of Peking, he was more patriotic than the British. He could not be tolerated by official diplomacy, and because of his outspoken views against the conduct of the campaign, he incurred official displeasure and fell foul of international politics. The American diplomats and officials close to Chiang Kai-shek distrusted these British attempts to regain their colony. Nor could the War Office in London understand this kind of patriotism. Even before the dramatic dénouement of the Pacific War at Hiroshima and Nagasaki, Ride's BAAG had been shunted into a relatively harmless position. The commandant was literally given the 'run-around' by the US Air Force, when he tried to persuade American planes to land him at Kai Tak. He finally consoled himself by returning to Hong Kong just in time for the official Japanese surrender, signed and delivered in the refurbished Government House on 16 September 1945.

Hong Kong at that time was not the anomaly it became in the post-war years—an enclave of stability and prosperity in a sea of political turmoil and poverty. But the historian cannot complete the story of this anguished period in Hong Kong's history without suggesting how easily that new world might not have come into existence.

Hong Kong's captive years began with a 13-day overture of fire; they ended with a similar postlude. The pride of Japan was finally crushed by the Tokyo fire-bomb raids and the two atomic attacks. The Japanese emperor's unprecedented prescript, accepting unconditional surrender, was issued on 14 August 1945.

In Hong Kong, that almost unbelievable announcement was accepted by the Japanese commanders a few days later. At that time, there was only a reduced and enfeebled British administration, and one person to whom the Japanese could surrender, Sir

Franklin Gimson, then a prisoner of war at the internment camp at Stanley. Local Chinese armies, hearing the news of the Japanese surrender, prepared to march into Hong Kong to receive the local laying down of arms on behalf of Chiang Kai-shek. The British were in a difficult position as their nearest forces were a small naval squadron under US command off the Philippines.

Meanwhile Chiang was following up his wartime representations to the Allies, and to Britain in particular, for new negotiations over Hong Kong's future. The Americans were not favourably disposed to the restoration of European imperialism in the area. If Franklin D Roosevelt had lived beyond April that year, the final outcome might have been very different. Hong Kong might have become an international city under the aegis of the newly created United Nations Organization. But Roosevelt was dead, and Churchill, determined not to preside over the liquidation of the British Empire, was no longer the British prime minister. After a flurry of telegrams at the highest level, Clement Attlee, Churchill's successor, managed to persuade the pragmatic Harry Truman to outface the Chinese head of state. Surprisingly, Chiang pressed his claims no further. The way was open for Rear Admiral Cecil J Harcourt, commander of the British naval squadron, to leave the US fleet and sail into Hong Kong on 30 August 1945—a fortnight after Emperor Hirohito's submission to the Allies.

Rear Admiral C J Harcourt, commander of the Allied Task Force to Hong Kong, making a radio address to the Hong Kong population.

The remaining token Japanese forces seemed prepared to make a last-minute stand for torpedo-boat bases on Lamma Island, but were soon neutralized. The British ships, the *Swiftsure*, the *Venerable*, the *Anson* and the *Euryalus* could then enter the harbour in safety.

A small assembly of locals greeted the liberators. There was cheering and rejoicing, but afterwards one truthful citizen admitted: 'To us it did not matter if the ships were American, British, Russian or Chinese. Whoever it was would be bringing food; at last we would eat again.'

As Japanese officers were evicted from the splendours of the re-named Peninsula Hotel, a British naval captain, Captain Eccles, and his staff occupied their suites and began issuing orders to mop up the frightened and bewildered Japanese units. It was also necessary to give them some measure of protection against the pent-up wrath of the local population.

In the Hongkong and Shanghai Bank, a document was later found which had been drawn up by a small group of Japanese administrators, asking their new masters for clemency and the right to settle with their families in Hong Kong. Of course, this request received short shrift. There were also a few other victims of the war during these last days of uncertainty. The Japanese gendarmerie were no longer feared, there were precious few colonial policemen fit enough to take up duty again, and the British Third Commando Brigade had not yet arrived by sea from Colombo. The local population was desperate for their share of the spoils of war, and public buildings and empty homes which had survived the hazards of the occupation were systematically stripped by gangs of looters. When the British troops landed and entered the city, there were many buildings which had been reduced to empty shells. Hong Kong would have to be rebuilt in the years to come.

30

31

32

33

34

35

36

37

38

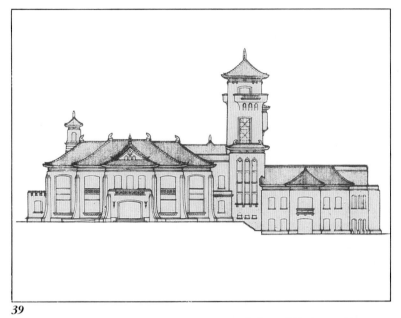

39

41

40

42

43

44

45

46

47

48

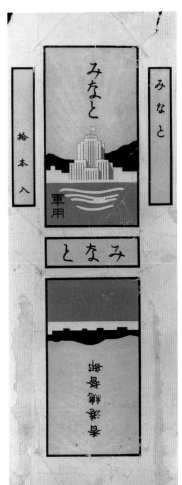

50

49

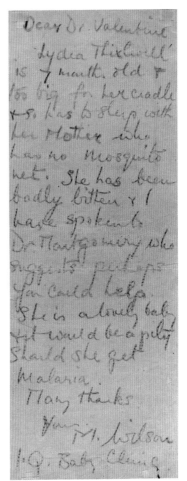

51

EXTRA

FLEET ENTERING

The first communique from the Hongkong Government to the people of Hongkong since December 1941 was issued this morning at 11 o'clock as follows:

"Rear Admiral Harcourt is lying outside Hongkong with a very strong fleet. The Naval Dockyard is to be ready for his arrival by noon to-day.

"Admiral Harcourt will enter the harbour having transferred his flag to the cruiser Swiftsure which will be accompanied by destroyers and submarines.

"The capital ships will follow as soon as a passage has been swept.

"The fleet includes two aircraft carriers Indomitable of 23,000 tons, and the Venerable; the battleship Anson of 35,000 tons and carrying 10 14-inch guns, the Euryalus and the Swiftsure carrying 10 5.2-inch guns; the merchant ship Maidstone of 8,500 tons, the merchant cruiser Prince Rupert, Canadian registry, and the Hospital ship Oxfordshire.

"A considerable number of other ships will follow in a day or two.

"The formal surrender is likely to follow the proceedings at Tokyo."

(South China Morning Post and The Hongkong Telegraph)
AUGUST 30, 1945.

52

53

54

55

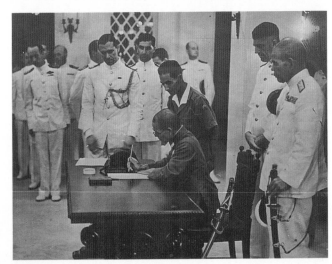

56

57

58

59

60

61

62

63

64

65

Captions (pages 72-86)

30   *Japanese bombers attacking Hong Kong, 8 December, 1941*

31   *British gunners with Indian auxiliaries exercising on artillery emplacements, 1940*

32   *British Defence Forces awaiting the imminent Japanese invasion, 1941*

33   *British troops on manoeuvres in the New Territories before the invasion*

34   *9.2-inch Howitzer gun battery on Mount Davis*

35   *A detachment of Japanese troops attacking the colony in the New Territories, December 1941*

36   *As the Japanese crossed the border at Shenzhen on 8 December, 1941, and moved into Kowloon they left a trail of destruction behind them*

37   *The Japanese military presence on the streets of Hong Kong*

38   *Japanese field ambulance unit*

39   *Government House, built in 1855, was remodelled on the orders of the Japanese governor, Lieutenant-General Rensuke Isogai, to incorporate traditional Japanese architectural features*

40   *Japanese troops at the Royal Navy Dockyard, 1945*

41   *Japanese soldiers studying a Chinese and Japanese notice in a local money changer's shop*

42   *Poster issued during the Occupation urging the local citizens of Hong Kong to utilize radio callisthentics programmes*

43/45/47   *Civilians in Hong Kong (except Third Nationals) were rounded up in January 1942 and put in an internment camp at Stanley, Hong Kong Island*

44   *Canadian POWs in the Sham Shui Po Camp, 1945*

46   *The military prisoners of war were confined in camps at Sham Shui Po and Argyle Street, Kowloon*

48   *An expression of British patriotism during the difficult times of captivity*

49   *Boxing day supper, Stanley internment camp, 1942*

50/51   *A message to the outside world, requesting much needed medical supplies, smuggled out of Stanley internment camp in a Japanese cigarette packet*

52   *The liberation edition of the South China Morning Post, August 30, 1945*

53   *Ships from the British Pacific Fleet arrived in Hong Kong harbour, 30 August 1945, bringing the Japanese Occupation to an end*

54/55/56   *Rear Admiral C J Harcourt receiving the surrender by the Japanese commanders in Hong Kong at Government House, September 1945*

57/58   *The end of the war heralded the return of British law and order, as Japanese commanders were charged with war crimes, 1946*

59/60   *Victory Parade in Central, 1945. The occasion was marked by the presence of Chinese troops in Hong Kong*

61/62   *Raising the British flag at Stanley (above) and at Government House (below)*

63/64   *Vanquished Japanese troops rounded up for return to their homeland, September 1945*

HONG KONG INTERNATIONAL AIRPORT: KAI TAK

*H*ong Kong's main gateway to the world is not the port or the 'fragrant harbour' , but the legendary Kai Tak Airport. Everyone who has flown into Hong Kong will recognize the aptness of Robert Cottrell's description: 'Jumbo jets swoop low over the tenements of Hong Kong, past a Marlboro advertisement which stares at passengers from what seems to be just a few feet away, before landing on a spit of reclaimed land jutting into the harbour.'

Excluding novelty demonstration flights of hot-air balloons over Hong Kong in the 1890s, aviation first came to the colony in 1911 on a landing strip at Sha Tin overlooking Tolo Harbour. It has been pointed out that the future runway, reclaimed from Kowloon Bay, was excluded from the convention of 1898, for it did not exist then.

The area occupied by Kai Tak was originally planned as a kind of garden city under the shadow of Kowloon Peak. Kai Tak is a convenient ellision of the first names of the two Chinese land speculators and developers, Mr Ho Kai and Mr Au Tak.

Strangely enough it was not Kai Tak but the seaside resort, Repulse Bay on Hong Kong Island, which at one time seemed to be the likely spot for Hong Kong's first airport. In the 1920s, a French aviator, Charles de Ricou, proposed a service linking Guangzhou, Haiphong in French Indo-China and Hong Kong. His fleet

of seaplanes, bought as a World War I surplus lot, actually landed at Repulse Bay and Lai Chi Kok. But his request to the local colonial authorities to overfly the busy harbour was turned down on the grounds of potential espionage. So the Gallic enterprise never really took off as a practical business venture.

A few years later the Aero Club of Hong Kong was formed. It used a small landing strip at Kai Tak, constructed by the Royal Navy for its aircraft operating from the carriers HMS Argus and Hermes.

In March 1927, the Royal Air Force established its own base at Kai Tak, with matshed hangars and fewer than three dozen airmen, but the primitive facility burned down three years later.

World War II in Hong Kong began, it could almost be said, with a Japanese bombing attack on the airstrip at Kai Tak that put the entire fleet of RAF Vicker Vildebeeste torpedo bombers out of action. Ironically, during their 44-month occupation of the British colony, the Japanese set the course for the expansion of the airport facilities in the post-war years. Stone and rubble hauled by British prisoners of war from the walls of nearby Kowloon Walled City were used to construct two hard-surface runways.

Whatever plans the Asian conquerors may have had for Kai Tak were aborted in August 1945, when the Japanese Imperial Forces

surrendered. The Royal Air Force was ready to move in at the end of the month. Preliminary parleys between the Allied officers and the Japanese troops were conducted at White Cloud Airport in Guangzhou, not at Kai Tak in Hong Kong.

Kai Tak then resumed the role it had begun in the years before the war. In 1936, Pan American Airways were operating their trans-pacific service to the United States using flying boats, the famous Clippers. British Imperial Airways at that time also stopped in Hong Kong on its empire-girdling itineraries. Other European airlines coming to Hong Kong included Air France and Lufthansa. Hong Kong's links with China were also important; planes belonging to the Nationalist China National Aviation Corporation had evacuated upper-class Chinese families to Hong Kong on the eve of the war.

When the hostilities were over, the Royal Air Force Transport Command took over Kai Tak. At that time it consisted of a runway and

terminal facilities in a hut by the water's edge. Passengers checked in at the Peninsula Hotel in downtown Tsim Sha Tsui.

There was another plan germinating at the time . Expansion was not thought possible at the Kai Tak location. A site in the Yuen Long valley at Ping Shan (later the RAF station at Sek Kong) was surveyed for a runway of 6,000 feet. However the plan was abandoned, because of fears that it would not meet international standards. And so Kai Tak continued upon its path of expansion.

In 1947, the Civil Aviation Department took over the airport. At that time the apron had two runways of 4,755 and 4,686 feet, both too short and with insufficient load-bearing capacity for the four-engined, high-speed planes of the post-war period. Within the next decade, the jetliner would be making even greater demands on airport facilities throughout the world.

The colony slowly and agonizingly prepared itself for the jet age. In the early 1950s,

Sir Ho Kai, one of the partners in the Kai Tak Land Development Company, formed in 1924 to reclaim land for housing (preceding page); a British Imperial Airways plane at Kai Tak before World War II. This pioneer air service to the Far East was a forerunner of the British Airways route (above)

a decision was taken to build a single runway of over 8,000 feet. The Director of Public Works told the Legislative Council that this would involve razing the hills around Kai Tak, creating vast areas of reclaimed land, and spending $135 million, the largest outlay the colony had ever incurred. The amount of earth to be moved could have created a mountain 500 feet higher than the Peak on Hong Kong Island! When construction began in 1955, the project employed over 3,000 men per day. One of their significant deeds was to cut away from the overlooking hillside a boulder weighing over 1,000 tons engraved with the Chinese characters 'Sung Wong Toi'. This was believed to be a memorial, more than 600 years old, to a boy emperor of the Song Dynasty, whose court had fled southwards to escape the Mongols.

The new runway was completed in 1961 at a cost of more than £8 million. This was to be the first step in the upgrading of the terminal facilities, arrival and departure halls, and ancillary services. At the time, over 14,195 aircraft and just less than half a million passengers per year used these facilities at Kai Tak.

The next stage in Kai Tak's development was the replacement of the old terminal with a larger and more up-to-date range of facilities. When these were completed in 1962, Governor Black claimed that Kai Tak was, '. . . one of the most modern and best equipped airports in the Far East'.

Even then there were plans to extend the runway again, and in 1975 an 11,130-foot runway accommodating 747 jumbo jets came into use. The new terminal building, designed in the late 1970s to handle 720 passengers an hour was strained beyond capacity; more than 4,000 arrivals and departures per hour made Kai Tak an extremely busy place. So once again, another new terminal was built to replace the previous one. The present terminal has an hourly capacity of roughly 5,500 passengers, or over 20 million a year.

So rapidly has the volume of air traffic into Kai Tak expanded that the airport is running

Chek Lap Kok Airport Plan

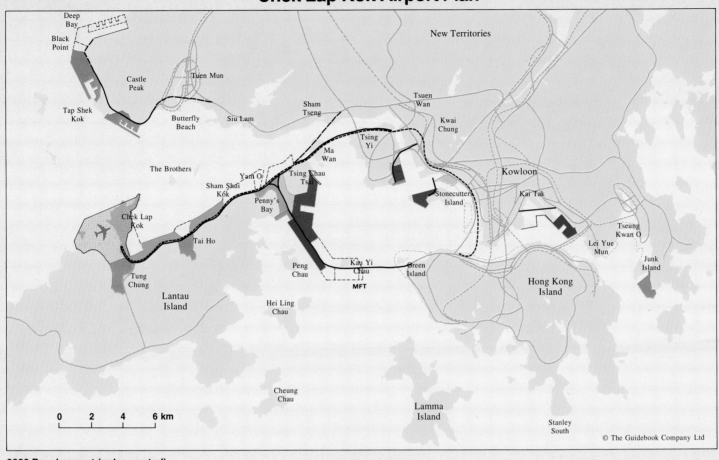

New Territories

Deep Bay
Black Point
Castle Peak
Tap Shek Kok
Tuen Mun
Butterfly Beach
Siu Lam
Sham Tseng
Tsuen Wan
Kwai Chung
Tsing Yi
Ma Wan
The Brothers
Yam O
Tsing Chau Tsai
Sham Shui Kok
Penny's Bay
Chek Lap Kok
Tai Ho
Stonecutters Island
Kowloon
Kai Tak
Tseung Kwan O
Lei Yue Mun
Junk Island
Tung Chung
Lantau Island
Peng Chau
Kau Yi Chau
MFT
Green Island
Hong Kong Island
Hei Ling Chau
Cheung Chau
Lamma Island
Stanley South

© The Guidebook Company Ltd

0   2   4   6 km

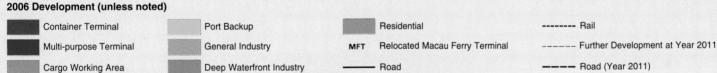

2006 Development (unless noted)

■ Container Terminal	■ Port Backup	■ Residential	-------- Rail
■ Multi-purpose Terminal	■ General Industry	**MFT** Relocated Macau Ferry Terminal	------ Further Development at Year 2011
■ Cargo Working Area	■ Deep Waterfront Industry	—— Road	---- Road (Year 2011)

out of space. In October 1989 the governor, Sir David Wilson announced plans for a massive Port and Airport Development Scheme, costing HK$127 billion. This was launched as an answer to Kai Tak's expansion limitations and as a local confidence booster post-1989. However disagreements between Mainland China and Great Britain over the project have protracted negotiations for nearly two years. Finally, in June 1991 both parties agreed to a Memorandum of Understanding, to be signed in Beijing later in the year, giving the go ahead for construction of a new international airport at Chek Lap Kok, Lantau.

The agreement has revealed an area of uncertainty with regard to the end of colonial rule and the high degree of autonomy promised in the Joint Declaration of 1984; it allows for greater Mainland Chinese intervention in Hong Kong affairs and dictates the financial parameters of the Special Economic Region, to in-

Opening of the new terminal, 1962 (preceding page, above); manually-operated arrival and departure board at Kai Tak Airport in the 1950s (preceding page, below); a modern-day view of the final approach to Hong Kong International Airport (left)

clude Hong Kong. But it is hoped that it will provide a solid base for local and international investment in Hong Kong and clear Chek Lap Kok's runway for an unimpeded take-off.

PART THREE

A Place in the Sun
Hong Kong's Struggle
for Survival 1946-66

*A city which in normal circumstances would be
well suited to house approximately one million people, is today
crowded by nearly twice that number.*

E Hambro, *The Problem of Chinese Refugees in Hong Kong,*
United Nations Report, 1955.

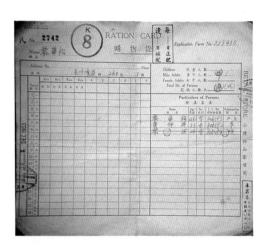

**Ration card, issued by the Hong Kong
administration, December 1953**

Hong Kong's existence is an accident in history. We have seen how Hong Kong might easily have passed back into Chinese hands in August-September 1945. During the following quarter of a century, the entrepôt port on the South China coast grew into an international metropolis. It might even be suggested, that it was the Chinese preoccupation with organizing a socialist state, which enabled the territory to work out a viable future for itself. If, at any time from 1950, when Chinese troops were massed on the border, even with the Hong Kong garrison at its largest ever, had the Chinese leadership decided to claim Hong Kong, there would have been no re-enactment of the Allies' defence of the Korean Peninsula. Hong Kong was recognized to be indefensible.

Ironically, it was the Korean War, the local focus for the international confrontation between communism and capitalism, which set Hong Kong on its course as the first rapidly industrializing economy in the Pacific region. The United Nations' 1952 embargo on exports to communist states shipped via entrepôts such as Hong Kong, gave further momentum to a process of industrialization which had its first impetus during the Sino-Japanese War (1937–1945).

Hong Kong's role as an international export base and financial centre was first conceived in the late 1940s and early 1950s. The treaty-port function, to serve as a channel for the movement of goods to and from China, was put on hold during this period, though it resumed a few decades later.

Hong Kong of course has never been completely cut off from China. Throughout this period, when Hong Kong was buffered, but not entirely insulated, from the disturbing currents of revolutionary and counter-revolutionary activities around it, this nucleus of neutral trade was continuously supplied with the necessities of life—rice, pork and vegetables from the Mainland. Later it was claimed that as these essentials had been supplied by China at subsidized prices, the territory's claim for consideration as a place of special economic value was weakened. Fortunately, this argument did not prevail and the productive symbiosis between agriculture in Guangdong and industry in Hong Kong has been recognized.

Needless to say, this symbiosis was long-standing and existed before the war. Guangzhou and Hong Kong were twin cities, some 120 kilometres (75 miles) apart, with regular railway and steamboat connections providing transport for money, goods and people. We have seen how, in the past, disturbances in Guangzhou and its surrounding hinterland would push the population of that area to move to the relative stability and prosperity of Hong Kong. And conversely, when there was trouble in Hong Kong, such as during the plague of the 1890s and the strikes of the 1920s, the population moved north. However, as Hong Kong struggled to stand on its own feet during the immediate post-war years, it was necessary to control immigration so as not to strain Hong Kong's resources.

Pre-war Hong Kong had survived on unrestricted access to markets and money. Immediately after the war it became part of the sterling area and subject to strict limitations (imposed by Britain) on the import of goods and export of capital. Had it continued to follow these strait-jacket mercantilist policies, it would never have recovered. Officials of the British Military Administration were shipped out to Hong Kong to run the liberated territory before the restoration of civil government and the return of Sir Mark Young as governor in May 1946. They were faced not only with the task of securing essential foodstuffs for the mounting population, but also with restoring Hong Kong's trade with China on a barter basis, though the potential here was limited. Eventually Britain released Hong Kong from its own long-lasting post-war restrictions on international transactions, and Hong Kong was economically free to embark again upon its venturesome trade policies.

It was possibly the security which Hong Kong offered through its courts and administration, rather than economic prosperity, which attracted the half-million Chinese immigrants who flocked to Hong Kong before the gates were closed in 1953. With this influx of immigrants, willing to endure a minimal existence (a squatter's hut on a roof or hillside, or a bed in a dormitory rented by the hour), Hong Kong was equipped for an industrial take-off unmatched in world history.

Before 1949, the culmination of the communist revolution in China, a number of Shanghai textile manufacturers had been considering Hong Kong as a new base for their operations. But it was only when the United Nations embargo on trade with China disrupted their plans for local expansion in 1950, that these entrepreneurs had their weaving machinery diverted to Hong Kong. 'Hong Kong Unlimited' was in business.

Chinese illegal immigrants (IIs) captured after crossing the border

Two essential human factors behind business success are entrepreneurial flair and labour. Hong Kong's industrial expansion was made possible by a pool of workers who put in long hours for little pay in cotton factories not unlike the 'dark satanic mills' of the Industrial Revolution. At first there was a preponderance of unmarried men not averse to living in factory barracks, where the basic necessities of food and shelter were provided. Later, as these workers established their families, they found accommodation in shanty towns such as Rennie's Mill, a relic of an earlier industrial establishment on the northern shores of Kowloon Bay.

This squatter population burgeoned not only in remote Kowloon Bay, reasonably close to the first of Hong Kong's satellite industrial townships, but also in Kwun Tong, an old fishing village submerged by a municipal tip for waste. Other communities grew up around the old industrial area near Lai Chi Kok in urban Kowloon, and at Aberdeen on Hong Kong Island. It was taken for granted by the local administrators that such homes lacked running water, proper cooking facilities and sanitation.

Thanks to significant developments in preventative medicine at this time, intensive inoculation programmes were implemented to prevent outbreaks of measles, polio, typhoid, cholera and tuberculosis. Thus it was possible to contain the health hazards created by a growing population without having to deal with the more fundamental element of city life—housing conditions.

The fire at Shek Kip Mei in 1953 was a catastrophe, but the mushrooming of many ramshackle settlements meant that squatter-hut fires became more common. Hundreds of timber and cardboard 'homes' disappeared in the blaze, and thousands of people were rendered destitute, forcing the government to rehouse them. As a result, a massive housing programme was developed, with the government as landlord; this now provides accommodation for half the population of Hong Kong.[10]

When the first resettlement blocks were built, government funds were so scarce that less than the minimal area needed by an adult could be provided (1.4 square metres or 15 square feet). Since then, as improved 'marks' of accommodation have been built, the standard has risen considerably, with a separate toilet, washing and cooking facilities, and separate sleeping areas in flats of up to 3.25 square metres (35 square feet) per person. This was as good as private accommodation for equivalent income levels.

The provision of public low-rent housing is a major exception to the constantly-stated policy of government non-intervention in the economy. The policy depended on the fact that the government did not take into account the putative price of the land for the estates when computing the cost of these investments.

Government intervention had another indirect influence in promoting industrial growth. There was genuine concern about the medical and safety problems generated by conditions in the squatter communities. But when the clearance of these pockets of 'free' accommodation was enforced, and the squatters were qualified to have quarters in the new blocks, these new tenants had to pay the government for water and electricity. In the squatter cantonments, power lines had been tapped by triad organizations, this being the only charge payable by the inhabitants. Sociologists, who have examined the economic and social adjustments made as a result of this official intervention, argue that it created an industrial proletariat. To meet higher living expenses, jobs in the new factories (with wages determined by the employers) had to be taken. This supply of cheap labour was an essential ingredient in Hong Kong's industrial expansion.

In the 1960s the streets of Hong Kong were thronging with farmers who had no experience of life in a city, wandering perplexed off the pavements oblivious to the danger of traffic. Until the 1970s, Hong Kong was a frontier town. In 1962, more than a third of its three million citizens were recent immigrants.

Hong Kong's growing population and lack of adequate housing in the 1950s left many families living on the pavement (above); Shek Kip Mei squatter-hut fire, 25 December, 1953 (below)

It was obvious that these waves of people, liberated from their bondage in the communes, could disrupt Hong Kong to the point of precipitating the collapse of the administration. Later population surges in the 1970s were to repeat the same strains, until the government belatedly introduced a strict policy regarding illegal immigrants.

Hong Kong Government officials discussing new housing programmes, 1960s

But this was a lesser danger. Among the refugees were the rich and middle class supporters of the Kuomintang. These capitalists started up businesses again in Hong Kong, running hotels, department stores and film studios. It should be remembered that communist China, during its waves of ideological reform, had purged the cities of private enterprise. Some of the shopkeepers and factory owners found havens in Taiwan and the United States, but the majority came to Hong Kong.

Then there were remnants of the contending armies of the civil war in China, abandoned by both sides. They would find a tenuous existence, still wearing the torn and filthy uniforms of their former allegiances, but living a ghost's life in the concrete shelters of Kowloon.

It was no surprise, therefore, that a relatively insignificant incident should flare up into the first of a series of three major disturbances—in 1956, 1966 and 1967—which punctuated the political history of this period.

The first incident in October 1956 lasted one month and was sparked off by rivalry between the two Chinese national days which occurred in that month. The red-letter day for the People's Republic of China was 1 October, while that of the Kuomintang in Taiwan was 10 October—Double Tenth. A small incident at the Li Cheng Uk Housing Estate in Kowloon, where an official removed the blue posters of Chiang Kai-shek, angered residents. The clash of ideologies burst into the open, despite government measures to suppress political demonstrations. The initial protest mushroomed into riots which spread throughout neighbourhoods from Tsuen Wan in the west to the airport in the east. By the end of the month, 60 people had lost their lives and several hundred more had been injured.

*Major bank runs of 1965 on Canton Trust,
Commercial Bank and Hang Seng Bank, the
first of several Hong Kong banking crises,
necessitated direct government intervention*

When the Star Ferry riots started in April 1966 in protest against a 5-cent rise in the first-class ferry fare, the first in 20 years, there was one lone demonstrator at first. So Sau Chung, an unemployed artist, had printed on his jacket an invitation to others to join him in his protest. A small number of sympathizers did so and there ensued a march along Salisbury Road in Tsim Sha Tsui. The Commission of Enquiry into the Kowloon Disturbances described this as the first peaceful demonstration in the history of the colony!

This expression of popular sentiment might have been confined to the ferry concourses if this had been the only grievance, and if the public had not been so offended by the action of the ferry company and of the government. The latter was blamed for other economic illnesses besetting Hong Kong at that time (1965 saw a series of bank crashes). Another wave of violence broke out, with looting and arson, probably whipped up by triad sympathizers of the right-wing political organizations. Again it was demonstrated that the densely-packed housing estates were ideal breeding grounds for riots. This time the number of casualties was considerably less, with one fatality. These riots featured the participation of youths who were unwilling to meekly accept changes proposed by the government.

Analysts blamed these events in part on the failure to meet rising expectations. Yet evidence was produced to show that even though the cost of living had risen over the previous six years at a rate of two percent, wage statistics had overtaken prices by six percent a year. In other words, the workers in the factories of Wong Tai Sin, San Po Kong, Cheung Sha Wan and Shek Kip Mei in northern Kowloon were gradually becoming better off.

The next outburst occurred only one year afterwards—such a short interval suggesting that certain forces in the social fabric were reaching breaking point. Further discussion of these disturbances, the most volatile in Hong Kong's history, is continued in the next section.

However, there was another critical factor in the recurrence of Chinese politics in Hong Kong. The central problem of Hong Kong's development, epitomized in the 1967 riots, had been foreshadowed in the disturbances that had taken place one year earlier. This was the gap between the people of Hong Kong and the government, the latter failing to bridge the gulf between what was seen as a privileged colonial elite ruling in a benevolent way, and the mass of the people.

The return of the civil government to Hong Kong in 1946 had been accompanied by a fanfare of social and welfare improvements. The lessons of the pre-war period, it was believed, had been learnt. The home governments, be they Labour or Conservative, were inspired by the salutary changes brought about by the war, in particular, a revolutionary regard for the welfare of the individual, often powerless to meet the vicissitudes of life, poverty, ill-health and poor education. They were willing to share this vision of a better life with their colonial subjects.

In Hong Kong, the embryonic departments dealing with these problems, symbolically but poorly represented by female almoners or public relations officers, were expanded to attend to the housing needs, working conditions and health of the working class. Their tasks were, as we have seen, multiplied by the sheer weight of numbers. There was another vital factor: Hong Kong was becoming a place of permanent residence, the home of the newcomers. Soon they would bear and bring up children here, with only lingering ties to the traditions of their native China. And before long their children would account for the majority of the population.

The proposed five-cent increase in the first-class Star Ferry fare in 1966 sparked off major riots in Kowloon

Governor Sir Mark Young, perhaps in peacetime less resolute than he had been in the dark days of December 1941, was responsible for initiating a thorough overhaul of the local administration. He replaced the ageing colonial mandarinate of Lower Albert Road, where the secretariat was situated, with the aim of involving the grassroots inhabitants in the running their own districts. These far-reaching reforms took about 20 years to implement. Today the District Boards, with their elected members, have limited fiscal powers to provide a sense of community and a decent, safe environment in the teeming resettlement estates.

From 1946 to 1949, this attempt was confounded by two main legacies of the past. The greatest obstacle was the fear of Chinese intervention. It was not until the Joint Declaration was signed in 1984, sealing Hong Kong's future, that the administration put this inhibition aside. From the late 1940s until the end of the Cultural Revolution, marked by the prosecution of the Gang of Four in 1976, it was feared that this volcano might erupt at any time. In that sense, the stabilization of Hong Kong depended upon the stability of China.

One can only speculate whether it would have been more beneficial to Hong Kong to be part of China and retain its own lifestyle, if that nettle had been seized in 1946-9, or to accept Governor Sir David Trench's local reforms in 1960s.

But the second legacy was unavoidable; it was part of Hong Kong's social fabric, rooted in the past. In the nineteenth century, liberal-minded governors had recognized the contribution of the Hong Kong Chinese merchants. Slowly they were incorporated into the legislative process where they could represent their own considerable interests. However, they became an 'establishment' in turn, leaving no room for lower ranks to voice the aspirations of the majority.

The Hong Kong Annual Report of 1956, one volume in the series giving the official version of Hong Kong's progress during the year (above); stamps issued in 1961 to commemorate the 50th anniversary of the founding of the University of Hong Kong (below)

In the 1930s, the Sanitary Board had been dominated by taipans, and from this the Urban Council had evolved. The Council took up some of the functions of the Sanitary Board, but it could never grow into a fully developed system of local government because of its very restricted franchise.

One of the arguments put forward against involvement was the difficulty establishing qualifications for local voters with a sufficient period of residence in the wards. In 1956, Sir Alexander Grantham was still lamenting the fact that the mass of people living and working in Hong Kong had no fixed stake in the colony. This colonial myopia blurred perspectives. The progressive administrators were unable to sort out the central and local principles of government; the Chinese establishment of senior Legislative Council members, jealous of their importance, did not require much persuasion to abort the Young Plan of reform in 1949.

This failure to institute political reform in Hong Kong, even on a municipal level, reflected a reluctance to found a welfare state. This was born of healthy misgivings about the efficacy of socialist programmes passed by parliament in Britain. The overriding aim of financial secretaries was to end the financial year with a surplus of revenue over expenditure in the government's current account. This aim was achieved every year after the war and in the immediate post-war period, except for 1959-60 and 1965-6 [11]. The second consequence was that, in the light of this Gladstonian fiscal wisdom, the government would not commit itself to programmes of social or environmental improvement which, if overseas economic conditions were to blight Hong Kong's own export earnings, might bankrupt the government.

Hindsight demonstrates that this Micawberish attitude was completely unfounded. The total value of trade did falter for a few years following the Korean War, but in the 1960s investment in manufacturing for exports began to pay ever-growing dividends. Unlike the earlier upheaval of the 1920s, not even the deeper-rooted disturbances of 1967 managed to halt this business boom.

The Hong Kong Government followed conservative policies; moreover, it was responsible for all the shortcomings of those policies which were shaped by market forces. The power of labour to determine wage levels was diminished by political divisions among trade unions, rendering them impotent as wage bargainers. No organized group, representing the needs of the ordinary worker or housewife, was able to put forward claims for a redistribution of income through policies yielding free education or social welfare benefits.

The number of children of school age had increased astronomically with the influx of permanent residents and the dramatic fall in infant mortality rates: by 1971 a census revealed that over 50 percent of the total population was under 25. A seven-year programme to build schools was started in 1954 to meet a 130-percent deficiency in the number of places, but at the end of that period, because of the population growth, there were still not enough schools. As the years passed, it seemed as if the Education Department would never catch up with the queues of potential students. In 1967, when the question of education became an immediate concern, the administration was alarmed to see that large numbers of children were attending left-wing schools offering free education. Here again a debilitating deficiency was revealed. Because the government had started from scratch, it had concentrated on the provision of free places only in primary schools. It was not able to offer compulsory free education at that grade until several years later.

Secondary education· lagged behind elementary. When a programme to build high schools was initiated at the beginning of the 1970s, there was provision in public schools for only 40 percent of the eligible age-group.

Hong Kong's economic development and industrialization were remarkable, mainly because of large-scale mass-production industries where technical skills were not essential. But it is clear that the reliance of the government upon market forces—the profit motive inspired private schools and evening colleges, with incongruous names like Eton and Harrow—was not ultimately to Hong Kong's benefit. This weakness was realized and the deficiency made up rapidly in the following decade.

Education in Hong Kong is most readily seen as a technical input into the production equation. The recent expansion of universities, technical colleges, polytechnics and the like has enabled Hong Kong to transform its industrial structure to higher-grade products, such as electronic goods. But by sharpening social skills and, belatedly, critical thinking, education has also played a part in facilitating the smooth running of a complex city.

Education was needed to give government administrative officers a deeper understanding of the changes in the territory they were administering. From this knowledge would spring a more profound understanding of the lives of the citizens. Hong Kong is, quite clearly, a volatile place where moods change rapidly. The riots of 1956 and 1967 proved how the aloofness and indifference of the Hong Kong administrator would put him wildly out of touch with local realities. Only a few dedicated district officers, who were genuinely concerned about the future of Hong Kong—in particular the New Territories—ever came close to their 'subjects'.[12]

There was some awareness in the 1960s that the Cowperthwaite strategy for dealing with Hong Kong's economic survival in a world of competition, of 'clearing the decks for action' (i.e. eliminating welfare considerations in the product function), was too shortsighted in its aims. In 1965 the government issued its White Paper on Social Welfare Aims and Policy which recognized, for the first time in Hong Kong history, the government's obligation to provide some form of social security.

But there was slow, begrudging acceptance of this principle. In the meantime, the slack was taken up by the voluntary agencies, which came to Hong Kong's rescue with housing, education, health and social care during those tempestuous years. In 1969, Financial Secretary Sir John Cowperthwaite softened to the extent of providing a minimal measure of relief for victims of typhoons, landslides and other calamities; but he was still as patronizing as ever. He repudiated 'the simplification that the people have to be given a reward, like children, for being good last year [the year of the riots], and bribed   . . . into being good next year'. Evidently, the willingness to consider such relief as necessary ingredients for social well-being and not as charity, was more a matter of principle than a lack of cash.

Sample products of Hong Kong's Industrial Revolution in the post-war period

The first stage of industrialization when products were hand-assembled, notably plastic flowers. Pictured here is a small vacuum flask factory

Throughout the 1960s, except for the temporary setback of the 1965 banking crisis, public revenue had risen annually. The expansion of the colony's economic and industrial structures necessitated the development of the infrastructure as well. There was an expanding demand for land, which was controlled by the government. Hence the proceeds from this source of revenue made it possible, as administration historian Norman Miners makes clear, to double the amount spent on social welfare by the early 1970s. But the Dickensian principle of 'less eligibility' adopted by the Hong Kong Government only accounted for one percent of the total budget. Even when the programmes introduced by the new governor, Sir Murray MacLehose, were put into effect, such benevolence only increased the burden on the treasury by up to two percent of total expenditure.

A big change of heart in government was inevitable. Hong Kong's growing prosperity was making the narrow concept of running Hong Kong in the Victorian mode more obsolete with each passing year.

To sum up, this period saw Hong Kong—slowly by its own measure of progress, but rapidly by world standards—putting itself together as an economic machine. The number of economically active people in the population increased from just over one million in 1961 to nearly two million in 1981. The workforce doubled in the manufacturing industries, chiefly in textiles. Whole new industrial areas came into existence, mainly in northern Kowloon. Fresh markets were being exploited; reliance on the desultory benefits of imperial preference, a legacy of the 1930s, was formally eliminated with Britain's entry into the Common Market in 1973, but Britain and its imperial territories had declined in importance as markets long before that.

Although such a suggestion might be discounted now with the threat of protectionism rising once again, it was fortuitous that Hong Kong's industrial progress coincided with the establishment of GATT in 1947. This international agreement effectively opened up wealthy markets, in particular the United States.

The concentration on manufacturing consumer goods, so eagerly bought up by a prospering Western world, has paid rich dividends to Hong Kong. The growth of the gross domestic product increased twofold in the critical decade of the 1960s. This enabled personal income to double as well (although, by 1971, this dividend was shared amongst a population which had grown by more than a third.) Moreover, that rate of increase has not only been maintained but has been cumulative. The prosperity of the 1970s and 1980s rested upon the foundations of the earlier decades.

In 1967, however, Hong Kong capitalists' contribution to the Motherland became a thorn in the side of the Red Guards. Indeed, it seemed as if this booming, speculating city was yet another example of imperialist exploitation, much like Shanghai had been in earlier days. And like Shanghai, it had to be brought to its knees.

This was the threat, both ideological and nationalist, hanging over Hong Kong. Hong Kong was vulnerable; even its colonial rulers in Britain might not have proved so resolute in resisting the clamour for the surrender of its ill-gotten territory. There were also dangerous rifts in society, in particular, the alienation of a large mass of citizens with no roots in the territory, who felt aggrieved at the minimal benefits handed out to them by employers. The year 1967 was to be a year of crisis for Hong Kong.

66

67

68

69

70

71

72

73

74

75

76

77

78

79

80

81

82

83

84

85

86

87

88

90

89

91

92

93

Captions (pages 103-114)

66 *Kowloon riots sparked off by a clash in ideology between Communist and Kuomintang sympathisers,October 1956*

67 *Hong Kong feels the effects of the final stages of the Communist Revolution on the Chinese Mainland, October 1949*

68 *British Forces leave Hong Kong for service in the Korean War, August 31, 1950*

69/70/71 *The 1952 United Nations' embargo on trade with communist states, principally Mainland China, together with the Korean War, gave Hong Kong industry the opportunity to develop. The influx of Shanghainese textile entrepreneurs was vital to the continuation of this growth period*

72 *View of Wanchai and Causeway Bay from the Peak, 1955*

73/74/75/76/77 *The New Territories were opened up for housing development in 1973 with Tsuen Wan, Sha Tin and Tuen Mun as the sites of the 'first generation' new towns*

78 *The physical trials of life in the burgeoning city. One extreme hardship was the water rationing of 1962*

79/80 *The Government of Hong Kong undertook successful health campaigns against cholera and other infectious diseases.*

81/82/83/84 *The Shek Kip Mei fire, December 1953, was a major factor in the initiation of squatter clearances and the development of the housing programme, financed by the government*

85 *Chinese customs post at the border (1860-1898)*

86 *The boundary stones between China and the New Territories, removed by the Japanese during the war, were replaced by the British and Chinese in 1949. Lo Wu, pictured here, is the Hong Kong border post and main entry point into China*

87 *Rounded up illegal immigrants (IIs) before their return to China*

88/89/90/91 *Since the early 1970s there has been a policy controlling the influx of immigrants from China. But the lure of Hong Kong has continued to attract significant numbers of IIs*

92/93 *Reclamation on Hong Kong Island began as early as 1842. The Central district underwent considerable land development in the 1950s, pictured here in 1956 and 1957. Reclaimed land provided the foundations for the City Hall complex and the new Star Ferry terminal*

PART FOUR

Sunset in the East
Hong Kong Returns
to China 1967-97

For us, too, the British Empire is past history.

Mr Edward Heath, at the Commonwealth
Prime Ministers' Conference, Singapore,
February 1971.

Paradoxically, the tensions, the strains and frustrations of life in industrialized Hong Kong, born of economic exploitation never made the communist solution to these social ills attractive to the majority of its population. It is significant that the flashpoints of 1967 were in the industrial areas, where conditions were harsh and employers intractable, as well as in the tightly-packed housing estates.

Tardy reforms were instituted by the government to ameliorate abuses and pressures during the 1960s. But they were also sources of further grievance. Attempts were made to limit the working hours of those thought to be incapable of protecting themselves: women, children and factory operatives. But their desperation to gain the only security they could achieve, their savings, made them greedy victims of their employers, who offered the bait of overtime pay to fill their overseas orders.

Even if working class families were the beneficiaries of the low-cost housing provided by a benevolent authority, their purchasing power was constantly being eroded by inflation. Without trade unions to bargain for them, they could not share in the prosperity of the booming economy. Confrontations in the factories between workers and management were inevitable.

The initial spark in May 1967 was the un-met demand of 600 workers at an artificial flower factory. The employers had given their classic response, to dismiss nearly 100 workers. The sequel was widespread sympathy strikes, demonstrations, clashes with the police and a death-toll of more than 50.

Maoist memorabilia of the 1967 riots in Hong Kong (preceding page, above); raid on Wah Fung department store in North Point, left wing headquarters during the 1967 riots (preceding page, below); students' protest (right); demonstrators storm the gates of the 'Imperialist stronghold', Government House, May 1967 (left)

This conflict was also brought to fever pitch by the intrusion of the Mainland factor. As Joe England and John Rear, commentators on Hong Kong's labour laws, point out: 'The disputes originated in workplaces with strong pro-communist elements, or involved left-wing unions, and they were characterized at the outset by the chanting of *The Thoughts of Mao Tse-tung*.' The Little Red Book was first used to inspire students at left-wing schools to run away with all the prizes at inter-school sports days. But as animosity grew in the streets, the revolutionary text, held aloft in clenched fists, became a banner of insurrection. An 'All Circles Anti-Persecution Struggle Committee', evidently modelled upon the messianic mobs of Red Guards across the border, took over the direction of the battle.

The committee was hectored by the Mainland newspaper, *The People's Daily*, 'to organize a courageous struggle against the British and to be ready to respond to the call of the Motherland for smashing the reactionary rule of the British oppressors'. It is impossible not to agree with England and Rear that the disturbances were 'a confrontation between one ideology and one nationalism against another ideology and alien rule, rather than a spontaneous eruption of long-felt discontent'.

Impressions of the troubled months from May to November took a deep hold in popular memory. There was menace in the air. The threat of a siege was highlighted by the appearance of blood-red pennants on the hillsides. Often the warfare was psychological as much as physical. The bombs were like huge fireworks, wrapped in red paper. They were the products of the leftist schools' chemistry laboratories, as was revealed when a young student blew himself up in a school near the Hong Kong University. Buses, trams and buildings were plastered with aggressive messages scrawled in ill-formed Chinese characters. It took a brave person to remove these defacements. Protestors clamouring around the Hilton Hotel in the Central business district, regarded as a capitalist bastion, liberally sprinkled themselves with red paint to impress spectators and photographers with alleged police brutality. It was the police, armed with their wicker shields and guns loaded with rubber bullets, who were in the frontline of the skirmishes.

Central Hong Kong experienced its own battle of opposing loudspeakers in Queen's Road, blasting out contending announcements from the Government Information Office

and the Bank of China building, bedecked with Chinese flags. The left-wing department stores, tourist markets for everything from cheap Mainland novelties to expensive works of art, became command posts for the demonstrators. In the daytime, these shops were avoided by locals who feared they would be secretly photographed for the dossiers of the Public Security Bureau in Beijing; at night, elaborate defences of booby-traps and ferocious spiked thresholds converted them into arsenals and military strongholds for the revolutionaries. At one point a store in North Point was dramatically stormed by the police, who were airlifted onto the roof by helicopter and took the rebels by surprise. After that demonstration of the effectiveness of the colonial police, the Bank of China thought it prudent to build an enormous wire cage over its roof to prevent such ungentlemanly tactics!

Another source of provocation towards the Chinese extremists were American servicemen frequenting the Wan Chai bars as part of their 'rest and recreation' leave from Vietnam. The naval dockyard, HMS *Tamar*, was used to refit the ships of the US Navy. At times it seemed as if Hong Kong would be invaded. One torrid day, a vast banner-swirling armada of fishing junks from neighbouring communes in the Pearl River estuary swept across the western entrance of the harbour in an unforgettable gesture of outrage at the presence of a US aircraft carrier.

The city was under siege from within. Hong Kong received most of its water from reservoirs in the hills of Shenzhen (Sham Chun). The supply dwindled to a trickle, providing a four-hourly flow every four days. This blockade, unlike that of 1941, was not a deliberate act to bring a parched Hong Kong to submission. Hong Kong's regimen of cold showers and clean laundry to beat the discomfort of those sultry days was in abeyance. Food supplies were also cut off for a period and the markets were empty.

A general strike was called in June; the left-wing unions were supported by a gift of $10 million from China to aid them in the struggle. The transport companies, in particular the Kowloon Motor Bus Company, were most affected by this call for solidarity. There were sporadic outbreaks of industrial action but the general strike never really took off. There were other echoes of the past, nonetheless. A boycott of the port, the ultimate weapon of persuasion, was called in July. Cargo ships were ordered not to enter Hong Kong; the local Seamen's Union attempted to dissuade their men from 'signing on' ships based in the territory. The boycott did have some effect. For a couple of months shipping in the harbour was disrupted. It was not until early September that the entry of four ships from China signalled the break in the boycott.

By then the fire had gone out of the local confrontations. The weather helped the police in the early days of May, when passions were at their highest and the protesters almost stormed Government House. The heavy summer downpours were nearly as effective as the police barricades in dispersing the demonstrators in Central.

The government rounded up extremists, prominent left-wing journalists and officials, and detained them in the Victoria Detention Centre. A dusk-to-dawn curfew kept people off the streets in the dangerous dark hours. In any case, the general reaction of the

*A raid on the workers' union headquarters
during the 1967 riots (preceding page, above);
home-made bombs used by the rioters
(preceding page, below);
there has always been fierce competition for
places at the University of Hong Kong (left)*

Hong Kong population was to stay indoors, put up the shutters and security gates and wait for the trouble to pass. Apart from the organized illegal rallies of the first period of confrontation, Hong Kong was quiet. It often seemed to be a dead city.

Police loyalty proved to be the key factor in arresting the surge of protest and violence. Thereafter, as the activists in Hong Kong were gradually disowned by the politicians in China, largely on account of their failures, the crisis began to simmer down. There were the sporadic bombs left on tramlines and on the steps of the Government Secretariat, still to claim lives late in the year. But by New Year 1968, the tremors which had shaken Hong Kong to its very foundations had passed.

The disturbances left several legacies. The first was to increase the 'distance' between the colony and Mainland China. It had been relatively easy for Hong Kong residents and tourists from elsewhere to have access to China before 1967. Afterwards, Hong Kong was cut off from Guangzhou and other cities in China. A wall of secrecy grew up around the People's Republic, and Hong Kong was a keyhole, but without a key to open the door. China-watchers peered through the tiny aperture in an attempt to decipher what was transpiring on the other side. Intelligence agencies set up a mobile television and radio receiver on Tai Mo Shan, Hong Kong's highest mountain in the New Territories, in order to eavesdrop on transmissions in Guangdong. As for the intrepid tourist, who only a year earlier could get on the train at Tsim Sha Tsui and travel across China, Russia and Europe and arrive at Victoria Station in London, the door to the Middle Kingdom was closed. Hong Kong was effectively sealed off from China.

After an interval of 25 years, a marked turning point in Hong Kong's relations with China was to come about only in the late 1970s with the reopening of the old channels by steamer, and with the development of new means of communication (the hydrofoil and aeroplane) to Guangzhou and beyond. Moreover, as China reopened its doors to tourists, local residents—naturally timid about venturing into the homeland—began to follow in increasing numbers to the newly-formed Chinese Special Economic Zones, at Shenzhen and Zhuhai, just across the border.

Commemorative coin to celebrate the opening of the Cross Harbour Tunnel, 1972 (left); opening of the Mass Transit Railway, 12 February, 1980 (right)

With the liberalization of China's economy after the Cultural Revolution, particularly the initiation of the Four Modernizations programme in 1978, the Hong Kong-China connection was revived. In addition to joint ventures in the Special Economic Zones, new hotels in Beijing and Guangzhou, and clubs and beach resorts for Hong Kong tourists, there was a process of backward integration in such areas as dairying and, more importantly, in the textile and garment industries. Workshops and households in southern China carried out the first, or lower-value, stages of manufacture, providing semi-finished goods to Hong Kong for export. Occasionally the process was two-way: foreign yarn was imported into Hong Kong, despatched to China to be woven and dyed, and re-exported to Hong Kong.

The port was now an industrial entrepôt and Guangdong was becoming Hong Kong's backyard. This integration led one economist to deduce that the frontier between Hong Kong and China was being washed away by the tides of economic development. This, of course, has not yet happened, even with new road networks to facilitate through traffic via the New Territories to Guangdong, and vastly expanded frontier crossing posts to accommodate convoys of lorries and trucks. Despite Hong Kong's future status as a Special Administrative Region, it is unlikely that the buffer area between the region and the Mainland will ever be abolished.

Not all of the enterprise originated in Hong Kong. China had long held controlling interests in several local import-export firms, as well as in the chain of China Products stores found throughout the territory. China had also invested in petrol stations and docking (container) facilities, to name just a few ventures. The Bank of China, the headquarters of Chinese financial interests in Hong Kong, operates the second largest network of branch banks. Symbolically as well as physically, its new office building, erected on the site of the oldest colonial structure in Hong Kong, towers over the new Hongkong Bank building on Queen's Road.

The 1970s in Hong Kong was a boom period, visible in the expanding and rising skyline. The New Towns programme was tentatively begun in the 1960s with Tuen Mun; but the construction of seven satellite cities with populations expected to rise to a total of 3.5 million by the turn of the century did not gain momentum until the 1970s.

Land in the New Territories was acquired by the government from the villagers of the decrepit old market centres, such as San Hui, Tai Po, Yuen Long and Sheung Shui. The demand to sell outstripped the government's capacity to pay for this former agricultural land, and so a lucrative system of credit developed. The villagers, on surrendering their ancient plots of paddy, were given 'Letters B', in effect, government promissory notes, with compensation payable in the future. Values soon rose and there was intense speculation. Sackloads of these valuable documents were bought up by development companies, bent on raising land values even further. The government naturally benefited. Land revenues could easily support a vastly expanded civil service to administer ever more elaborate forms of local organizations. The City District Office scheme was the immediate government reaction to bridge the perilous gap between the people and the administrators.

Increasingly the government poured money into the social and welfare services, in particular into education. A full system of compulsory free education, including secondary education, was in place by 1974. At the same time cultural facilities were inaugurated, along with the Hong Kong Arts Festival, which brought first-class international performers to the territory. A number of specialized museums and cultural centres were also opened. New schools and hospitals were built; Hong Kong's two universities (the most recent at that time being the Chinese University of Hong Kong at Sha Tin in the New Territories)[13] were complemented by two polytechnics. The government's housing programme was expanded by the construction of better-designed estates, which loom dozens of storeys high over the former rice paddies of the Sha Tin and Yuen Long valleys. A Home Ownership Scheme also came into existence with the aim of creating a band of lower-middle-class flat owners. This scheme was greatly subsidized by excluding the cost of land from the calculations of the price to be paid for flats of modest size.

It was innovatory, if not revolutionary, for a financial secretary, in this case Sir Philip Haddon-Cave, to proclaim the government's intention to improve the quality of life. Perhaps the most far-reaching decision was to put aside 40 percent of the territory as Country Parks, where the irreversible encroachments of the developers would be kept at bay. They would also, of course, provide lungs for the rapidly urbanizing areas of the New Territories and Kowloon, as well as water catchment areas for the reservoirs. The need for such recreational areas had long been recognized—scarcely any patch of natural greenery in the inner city areas has escaped the invasion of concrete. But it was the determination and enthusiasm of the then-governor, Sir Murray MacLehose, who had personally blazed a nature trail some 50 miles in length across much of the New Territories, which set a seal on the necessary legislation in 1976 to dedicate Hong Kong's 'precious' land to this purpose.

Such diverse involvement in the daily lives of Hong Kong citizens suggests that the government was serious in its intentions. Hong Kong was not quite a people's republic such as Singapore; but in its welfare provisions and degree of public investment it was well on the way to becoming like the more southerly city-state.

Commemorative stamps issued in 1981 to celebrate the public housing programme

IT was, indeed, a great moment in the life of Peter Fitzroy Godber. He had been honoured by the Queen with the Police Medal for meritorious service.

And Princess Alexandra, as the Queen's representative, was on hand to pin it to his chest.

It was October last year during the Hongkong visit of the princess – and it was a happy day for Chief Superintendent Godber.

But storm clouds were looming on his horizon. This week they broke. Now Superintendent Godber is missing – the subject of an anxious, intensive search by Hongkong's Anti-Corruption Branch.

GODBER'S MOMENT OF GLORY

Chief Superintendent Godber receives the Queen's Police Medal, before his dramatic downfall over charges of corruption

The development of Hong Kong's basic economic structure showed in many ways: there was growth in its manufacturing industries, updated by the more significant contribution of the electronics industry; it had expanded its physical infrastructure—the airport, container terminals for shipping, the two Cross-Harbour Tunnels, and the underground railway network of the Mass Transit Railway; it had built satellite towns and their connecting roads; and it now had a vital extension to its water supplies: an idle desalination plant, although Hong Kong is still reliant on China for much of its water. But Hong Kong's spectacular growth and prosperity again brought to the surface two dangerous threats—corruption and illegal immigration.

Both of these threats could be said to have their origins in China and both demonstrated to the world the possible dangers of Hong Kong's inescapable contact with the Mainland. The first, the problem of corruption in the civil service, the police and among the business community, had troubled the colonial administrations of Hong Kong almost from the beginning of its history. The prevailing ethic had been to ignore its existence despite all the evidence to the contrary. To attempt to eradicate this lubrication of office would create greater confusion than to let it run its prosperous course, provided it did not become too noticeable.

Occasionally, a local reformer, such as the redoubtable Elsie Elliott (now Mrs Tu), a missionary refugee from the Mainland, was so persistent that action had to be taken. Before Governor MacLehose had assumed office, the government had been content to leave the police force, the principal target of Mrs Elliott's attacks, to investigate its own abuses. In 1973, the government set up a commission of inquiry under the chairmanship of a supreme court judge, Sir Alastair Blair-Kerr. This led to the establishment of the Independent Commission Against Corruption (ICAC) the following year; its task was to root out the corruption gripping almost every institution. Jack Chater, a respected civil servant of integrity, and later chief secretary, took charge and went about his task with a missionary zeal, striking terror into the hearts of the police divisions—at one time, about half of the Kowloon force was under suspension pending investigation.

The matter became so serious that in October 1977, a small but significant group of police officers stormed the headquarters of the ICAC. There were even fears that the mutiny would spread and that Government House would be besieged. It was only after the governor managed an about-turn on the eve of an expected announcement regarding further stern measures, that the crisis was defused. An amnesty was declared for acts of corruption committed before 1 January 1977, except in cases where warrants had been issued. The police, the vital key to stability in a period of mounting crime, were politically appeased.

The second threat was another intensification of a running-sore problem—illegal immigration. As the late David Bonavia, former correspondent of *The Times,* pointed out, 'MacLehose's achievement was to link it with legal immigration from China'. In the 1960s and early 1970s, when the industrial and construction sectors were experiencing a labour shortage, the constant flow of Cultural Revolution refugees could be dealt with leniently. This was the era of the 'touch base' policy: if an immigrant from China managed to reach the city's urban area, he or she could become eligible for a certificate of identity granting residence in Hong Kong.

But the crowding of Hong Kong with IIs (illegal immigrants) was making life difficult for longer-term residents. It was estimated that for every II caught and repatriated, two or three others qualified for legal recognition. In 1979 there were nearly 80,000 legal immigrants in Hong Kong, and another estimated 180,000-270,000 IIs. Accompanying this surge was a mounting wave of violent crime as the IIs turned to the only available way of making money. Soon this criminal activity would be organized by syndicates on both sides of the border.

Less noticeable, except to the administration, was the growing pressure on housing, social welfare services and the police. It was, as Bonavia said, 'a truly awesome prospect for a government already fighting problems of overcrowding, crime and public amenities'. There could only be one outcome, although it had long been delayed through Hong Kong's tradition as a place of refuge. In 1980 the 'touch base' policy was abandoned. Intensive and rigorous stop-and-search police operations were mounted and those who 'snaked' through the reinforced wire fences at the border and were caught, were returned under police escort, thus reducing the numbers to more manageable proportions. Tragically, however, this wave of migration by land coincided with the mass exodus of Vietnamese boat people from their communist-dominated homeland.

The problem of how to deal with the boatloads of refugees from war-torn Vietnam has presented the government of Hong Kong with its worst dilemma. The problem has been not just one of numbers, nor can it be compared to the influx of Chinese. There has only been one short period when China, as an act of political retaliation, has refused to take back its own citizens attracted by the Hong Kong magnet of prosperity and freedom. That was in September 1989 when Hong Kong allowed the Chinese swimmer Yang Yang, a potential victim of post-Tiananmen prosecution, to leave the territory for the United States, instead of being returned to China as the Chinese authorities insisted.

The influx into Hong Kong of boatloads of seaborne would-be migrants from Vietnam, anxious to secure United Nations' endorsement and further passage to their final intended destination in the West, has assumed alarming proportions. Presently, despite limited voluntary repatriation, the numbers have mounted. 1989 was the year of crisis, when arrivals exceeded 34,000; the highest figure for a decade, bringing the year's total number of uninvited guests to over 50,000.

The first influx of early Vietnamese boat people arriving in the territory

The British Government's aims in their negotiations with the Vietnamese Government were not so much to restrain the departure of the refugees from Vietnam, but to arrange for them to be repatriated. It appears that the Vietnamese Government is cynically using their own people as pawns to exact compensation from Britain and the international community, in particular the United States, and, as yet, has made little attempt to curb the exodus. Each spring the sailing season brings the barely sea-worthy craft and the promise of a recurring nightmare for the Hong Kong administration.

Local demonstrations against attempts to house the boat people reveal how the administration is flying in the face of a growing number of citizens, by continuing 'the right of first asylum policy'. This prevents the Hong Kong Marine Police from turning away the

Mandatory repatriation triggers off demonstrations in the closed camps holding the Vietnamese boat people (above); Christmas card made by Vietnamese boat people in the camps, 1990 (below)

boatloads of people at sea and forcing them to find other destinations in the region. This policy is 'dictated' to Hong Kong by Britain, exercising its foreign-policy prerogative over the colony. In 1989 a number of Vietnamese boat people were literally dumped on a remote island in Hong Kong waters and provided with the barest provisions and most basic amenities. This is because the overcrowded, hastily-constructed camps in the New Territories, where the Vietnamese boat people had been confined, had become flashpoints for violence and disease.

The government has followed a course of austere humanitarianism. The closed-camp policy of keeping the refugees behind barbed wire was intended as a deterrent to other would-be migrants. The failure of this policy is evident from the pressing numbers who continue to come, and the general indifference of the rest of the world (including Britain) who have decided to treat these suffering souls not as political refugees fleeing from oppression, but merely as 'economic migrants'. The only effective solution is international co-operation. And Hong Kong, which bears the brunt of the problem, is almost as much a victim of the situation as the refugees themselves. There are as yet no clear signs of a breakthrough in the negotiations between the principal parties, Britain and Vietnam.

Some of the refugees have been persuaded to volunteer for repatriation, but the response has always been minimal. Official targets have not been met and the vast majority of Vietnamese boat people remain in Hong Kong awaiting salvation by means of transfer to other holding camps overseas or preferably permission to settle in their preferred destination.

In June 1988, the government introduced a policy of screening arrivals to determine genuine refugee status. This only aggravated the situation. This policy was challenged by some Vietnamese boat people who sought redress against inadequate investigations. In December 1989, the Hong Kong Government, with the consent of London, attempted a desperate remedy. This was to adopt the policy of mandatory repatriation, which the negotiations at Geneva a few months earlier had refused to endorse. Hong Kong, faced with mounting friction in increasingly crowded camps, plucked out a mere 51 boat people (mostly women and children) and bundled them out of Hong Kong by plane in the middle of the night. In the event, this course of action quickly demonstrated its dangers: it provoked an international outburst of condemnation.

Despite the spectacular economic developments which were so attractive to the IIs, Hong Kong underwent a severe recession as a result of the 1973 world oil crisis. This was followed by a dangerous level of speculation in land and development and a high rate of inflation rocketing the colony into a boom or bust situation. This was a time, too, when wise business leaders were diversifying the local economy into local banking and financial services.

The building boom revealed a reckless or over-optimistic view of the economic growth by bankers and investors alike. This was exemplified by the bizarre and extraordinary inventiveness displayed by the builder of the Carrian empire, George Tam, who created empty financial empires from fictitious assets. Even the pillars of Hong Kong's financial sector, the Hongkong and Shanghai Bank and the Hong Kong Land Company, which transformed Central district into an integrated modern business area, got caught up in the fever and subsequently suffered financially.

This surge of speculation and development again raised the question of what arrangements would prevail after the expiry of the lease on the New Territories in 1997? The two-year period of negotiations which began with Margaret Thatcher's visit to Beijing in September 1982 and ended with her subsequent signing of the Sino-British Joint Declaration in 1984, was as crucial as any period in Hong Kong history.

It is difficult to imagine the five or six million inhabitants of Hong Kong remaining indifferent to the outcome of the frequent talks involving the British ambassador in Beijing and his adviser, the governor of Hong Kong, with the Chinese leaders. Hong Kong's part, immaculately orchestrated by the British Foreign Office, was to accept the framework of confidentiality. This left the negotiatiors' hands untied enabling them to accept the the repetitive brief communiqués of 'useful and constructive' announced by the governor. The latter was not really a party to the negotiations; these were strictly between China and the United Kingdom. Hong Kong was the meal on the table, to be disposed of as quietly as possible. The Chinese holding the upper-hand announced a termination to the feast.

In Hong Kong, with the conclusion of negotiations, there was a vague process of consultation, not a referendum, with Hong Kong's 'citizens' after the publication of the Draft Agreement in September 1984. An Assessment Office was created in Hong Kong. Two independent monitors, Sir Patrick Nairn, an Oxford lawyer, and Mr Justice Simon Li Fook-sin, representing Hong Kong, were appointed to oversee and report upon this collection of reactions to the historic settlement. Their report, which was published after a formal debate in the Legislative Council, found the agreement acceptable.

There was no practical alternative. This passive acceptance grew out of the recognition that ethnically Hong Kong was over 96 percent Chinese. A Unilateral Declaration of Independence, as proclaimed in earlier years by Rhodesia, was unthinkable. All Hong Kong could do was to express its anxieties—especially over China's right in an emergency to maintain civil order by stationing garrisons of the People's Liberation Army in Hong Kong.

This feverish period in Hong Kong's history sent shock-waves through Hong Kong's economy. The measure of its stability, the dollar, tumbled to a record low against the currency of its major trading partner, the United States. The result was 'historic' in that the agreement was reached years ahead of the contingency it provides for in the future.

Most important, Hong Kong was to be a Special Administrative Region under the jurisdiction of a Basic Law or 'mini-constitution'. 'The Hong Kong Special Administrative Region would enjoy a high degree of autonomy, except in foreign and defence affairs.'

Outlined were provisions for Hong Kong to have its own executive government. However, China could nominate the chief executive upon consultation with the Hong Kong people or its elected representatives. The document also guarantees the fundamental liberties 'of the person, of speech, of the press, of assembly

The Prince and Princess of Wales' four-day visit to the colony, 1989 (above); Governor Sir David Wilson announces the Port and Airport Development Scheme to members of the Legislative Council in his annual policy speech, 10 October, 1989 (below)

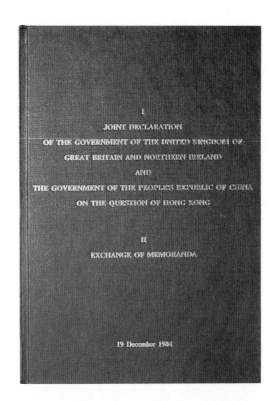

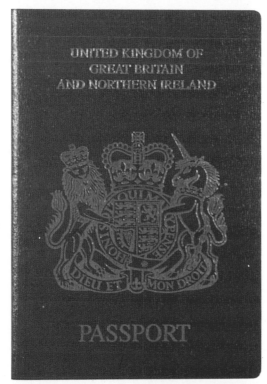

Joint Declaration of the Government of the United Kingdom of Great Britain and Northern Ireland and the Government of the People's Republic of China on the question of Hong Kong, 19 December, 1984 *(above); the new British National Overseas passport issued in July 1987 to Hong Kong citizens will replace the Dependent Territories passport after 1997 (below)*

. . . of travel, of movement, of correspondence, of choice of occupation, of academic research and of religious belief'.

The joint determination was that the current social and economic systems of Hong Kong would remain unchanged according to a 'one country, two systems' concept for a period of at least 50 years. As Governor Sir David Wilson has said: 'Hong Kong is linked to China, but, in another important sense, separate from it.'

The Joint Declaration was a document setting out agreed principles and intentions for the future. From this remarkable fruit of diplomacy, Hong Kong's population is supposed to derive hope for the years to come. But as the people of Hong Kong know better than anybody, the future cannot be guaranteed in writing. The Declaration specified China as the destination for Hong Kong, but there are no charts to give warnings of the shifting tides and shoals to be encountered on the way.

The touchstone of sovereignty for the ordinary citizen in Hong Kong had already been diminished by the previous erosions of the British Dependent Territories passport. Since 1981, Hong Kong holders of British passports no longer had the freedom—possibly regarded as an integral bond between Britain, China and the dependent territory—of the 'right of abode' in the homeland.[14]

The severing of constitutional links between London and Hong Kong has not been worked out as yet. Constitutionally the culmination will be the change in the legal status of the governor, presently the British sovereign's representative in Hong Kong. In 1997, not only will the official parades and the cockatoo plumes disappear but also all the little-known instruments of legal power vested in the governor. The man in the street will not be interested in these constitutional technicalities. The 1997 handover will focus on the kind of person to be nominated as governor. Will he be a communist party official from afar, like the provincial mandarins of imperial China, or will he be a local figure-head representing Hong Kong's international business and culture? Perhaps by then the anachronistic seat of authority, Japanese-built Government House, where the royal arms are displayed and the Union Jack flies, will be obsolete.

The British Government's presence in Hong Kong will be reduced to the occupancy of a building with a brass plate on the door that reads 'H M British Consul-General'.

It is difficult for the historian to see the events of the years after 1984 in perspective. Some of the events affecting the territory in its final years as a British dependency reflect increased uncertainty. For instance, in 1984 China made the decision to construct China's first nuclear power station at Daya Bay just across the border. In 1986, more than a million Hong Kong residents signed a petition, later presented to Beijing, objecting to the plan on account of the radiation risk to the population in the event of an accident. Britain was keen to supply the generating equipment instead of France for the US$4 billion nuclear facility. Some local legislators were afraid to rock the boat by voicing local concern over safety and thus China was able to dictate the terms of the contract—Hong Kong would buy 70 percent of the electricity generated from China. As Kevin Rafferty, author of *City on the Rocks: Hong Kong's Future* argues, here was another example of 'China's determination to get its own commercial interests first and of local legislators' unwillingness to stand up to Beijing'.

Popular concern was substantiated in 1987 when it was discovered that a significant number of reinforcing bars had not been installed in the reactor's foundation, leaving it below the required safety standard. Could the Hong Kong people trust the concern or competence of the supervising Chinese authorities who, whilst claiming that their management of this construction was very good, admitted that this was an example of '. . . quality control which still lacks perfection'. In the light of this confession, one might be pardoned for thinking that the political risks for the future were minor in comparison!

The other tremor which started outside of Hong Kong but which nevertheless shook the territory's economic foundations to the core, was the October 1987 stock market crash. As the news from Wall Street hit the Tokyo Exchange, Hong Kong's Hang Seng Index plunged from over 4,000 to below 2,000 points. Moreover, in their reaction to the shock, the extremely small number of businesses controlling the Hong Kong Exchange panicked. The Exchange was closed for four days, officially to allow the outstanding transactions to be sorted out, but also benefitting local brokers at the expense of overseas investors.

The Hong Kong Government, which agreed to this unprecedented act, later bailed out or at least cushioned several financial institutions and individual investors. This was not an unprecedented action, but this episode made it clear that the administration was ill-equipped to solve an endemic problem which is growing increasingly acute. It now appears caught between the dilemma of following the habitual approach of apparent non-intervention and thus risking an irreversible collapse of confidence in Hong Kong's stability or being drawn into rescue operations, some of which are of questionable public interest.

Hong Kong suffered another loss in December 1986, the death in Beijing of Sir Edward Youde, the highly respected governor during the period of the Beijing negotiations. He had managed to instill a feeling of calm and quiet confidence during those critical years when Hong Kong's future was at stake. Youde, popular as an unassuming and highly efficient administrator in Hong Kong, was trusted by the people despite his difficult role. (Officially he was snubbed by the Chinese because Hong Kong had no voice in the negotiations.) To Britain, and the Foreign and Commonwealth Office, the implementors of foreign policy, he played the plausible anchor-man role and reported to his voteless constituents in Hong Kong that the progress made in the 22 negotiating sessions in Beijing was 'useful and constructive'. So much so, that when an unpessimistic survey of Hong Kong opinion on the Joint Declaration was published in a 1989 book entitled *Hong Kong Voices*[15] almost all of the 30-odd respondents expressed some optimism about the post-1997 arrangements. Even the few interviewees who were critical of the Joint Declaration could not publicly denounce it; they contented themselves with mild reservations about Chinese intentions.

Youde's successor, Sir David Wilson, also a Foreign Office man, arrived in Hong Kong in April 1987. His job was seen as one of overseeing the diplomatic moves leading to the convergence of two ideologically opposed systems. His task was also to build up hope for Hong Kong, principally by offering the prospect of an accelerated rate of democratization and transformation of the old colonial system of government. (Even before Sir Edward Youde's death, the government was anxious not to appear as a lame duck administration.)

Even children participated in demonstrations against the Basic Law, April 1990 (above); the flag of the future Special Administrative Region (Hong Kong), which will fly at mastheads of the former British colony from July 1997 (below)

Local support for democracy in Mainland China at Happy Valley racecourse, immediately after the Tiananmen protests in Beijing, June 1989 (above); local citizens demonstrate against Britain's refusal to give the right of abode in the United Kingdom to 3.25 million British Dependent Territory citizens in Hong Kong (below)

With Sir David's arrival, and especially after the events of May-June 1989 culminating in the Tiananmen Square massacre, it seemed as if Hong Kong and Britain were going to put aside the long-standing caution towards democratic aspirations in the colony. The governor affirmed, 'Our own laws are freedoms which we cherish. They must not be eroded'.

At the same time, a costly and adventurous programme was announced. It involved the public in the infrastructure for a new Hong Kong; there would be a new port, a two-runway airport, and a massive integrated system of roads, tunnels and bridges linking Hong Kong's outer islands.

But overshadowing these ventures was the impending final round of talks to formulate Hong Kong's constitution for the 50 years after 1997. The Basic Law, a part of Chinese law, would place Hong Kong under the direction of the National People's Congress in Beijing. The responsiveness of the makers of the Basic Law to the fears and aspirations of the people of Hong Kong, as parochial and unformulated as they might be, were reflected in the promulgation on 4 April 1990. This set the tone decisively and irrevocably for the remaining seven years of British rule. After the Tiananmen massacre, the people of Hong Kong saw the danger lights ahead; with the promulgation of the Basic Law the end of the road for the British-designed and operated vehicle—colonial, capitalist Hong Kong—is evident for all to see.

94

95

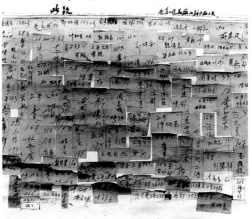

96

97

98

99

100

101

102

103

104

105

106

107

110

108

109

111

112

113

114

115

116

117

堅決
支持中國學運
反對軍事鎮壓
爭取民主自由

再見！一人政治！

118

119

Captions (pages 131-140)

94/95/96   The 1967 riots were Hong Kong's reaction to the Cultural Revolution on the Mainland. The confrontation took the form of labour disputes, bomb outrages and a propaganda war of words

97/98   The paddy fields of the New Territories were overlaid by the concrete of the new towns. Contrast a rural scene in Sha Tin with the satellite towns of today

99   Governor Sir Murray MacLehose, (1971-1982), unveiling a plaque to commemorate the opening of one of the housing estates in the Home Ownership scheme, May 1981

100 Completion of the electrification of the Kowloon—Canton Railway to Lo Wu in July 1983 shortened the journey time to China considerably

101 View of the Special Economic Zone of Shenzhen from the Hong Kong border

102/103/104/105/106   From 1972 onwards, Vietnamese refugees flooded into Hong Kong seeking asylum. In 1988 a screening policy was introduced to determine whether they were ` political refugees or economic migrants. Mainland China has stated that there should be no Vietnamese refugees in the territory at the hand-over in 1997

107/108/109/110/111   Negotiations concerning the return of Hong Kong to China began with British Prime Minister Margaret Thatcher's visit to Beijing in 1982. After subsequent visits by Sir Geoffrey Howe, her British Foreign Secretary, the terms of a Joint Agreement were outlined. The final document, the Sino-British Joint Declaration, was signed in December 1984 by Prime Minister Thatcher and the Prime Minister of the People's Republic of China, Zhao Ziyang

112/113/114   Local residents demanding the right of abode in Britain during the arrival of visiting British Foreign Secretary Sir Geoffrey Howe, at Hong Kong International Airport, 2 July, 1989. Protest gatherings were also staged outside the residence of Government House and the New China News Agency

115/116/117   The impact of Tiananmen Square (1989) in Hong Kong and memorial demonstrations one year later in Victoria Park

118/119   Post-Tiananmen posters protesting against the events and communist personalities in China

TOWARDS DEMOCRACY

As a Crown Colony, Hong Kong's constitutional system derives most of its authority from the Royal Prerogative. Letters Patent authorize Her Majesty's Representative, the Governor (the Governor in Council taking the advice of the Executive Council and the law-making body, the Legislative Council), to rule the colony.

In the past this has both constrained all attempts to reform the legislative system and confounded proposals to democratize the outmoded colonial structure. It is one of the arguments of this book that the granting of self-government has always been ruled out by Britain; chiefly from a belief that any reform, in particular the granting of independent responsible government, would so upset China (in particular after the establishment of the People's Republic of China in 1949) and would put the future of the colony in jeopardy. Thus the introduction of a system of popular representation to the legislative body through elections has

been delayed. Although there have been some modifications of this iron rule in the past decade, the matter of direct elections to these bodies has not been fully resolved. This has also meant that, until recently, it has been difficult to separate the functions and accountability of the central and local governments.

The only historical exception to this state of affairs, dating back to the pre-war period, is the Urban Council. This council is the direct descendant of the Sanitary Board of the 1880s and was, as late as the early 1970s, drawn from a very small body of some 34,000 electors. The rationale given for this oligarchic situation was the general political apathy of the Hong Kong people, reinforced by the fact that the functions of the Urban Council were indeed municipal. However, the central government collected the rates to enable the Urban Council to carry out its modest functions of supervising such matters as markets, beaches, hawkers, cem-

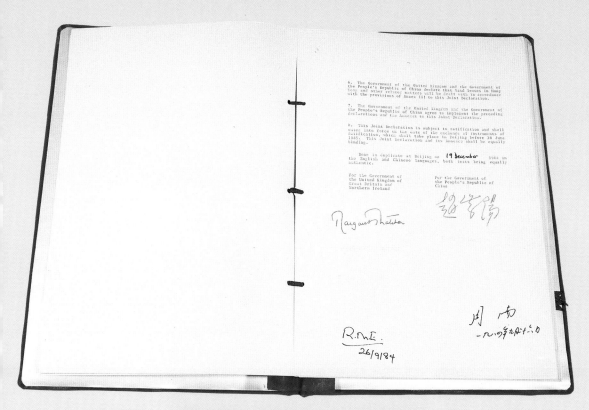

6. The Government of the United Kingdom and the Government of the People's Republic of China declare that land leases in Hong Kong and other related matters will be dealt with in accordance with the provisions of Annex III to this Joint Declaration.

7. The Government of the United Kingdom and the Government of the People's Republic of China agree to implement the preceding declarations and the Annexes to this Joint Declaration.

8. This Joint Declaration is subject to ratification and shall enter into force on the date of the exchange of instruments of ratification, which shall take place in Beijing before 30 June 1985. This Joint Declaration and its Annexes shall be equally binding.

Done in duplicate at Beijing on 19 December 1984 in the English and Chinese languages, both texts being equally authentic.

For the Government of the United Kingdom of Great Britain and Northern Ireland

For the Government of the People's Republic of China

eteries, crematoria, libraries and cultural and popular entertainment in the urban areas. It has its own City Hall and a chairman, elected by councillors from the membership (themselves either officially appointed or elected by constituencies), was popularly regarded as the 'Mayor of Hong Kong'. This was the case under the energetic leadership of Mr A D O'Sales.

In the New Territories there was another relic of the past—the Heung Yee Kuk. This council was set up early in this century to represent the interests of the indigenous villagers of the leased area. Village representatives and village elders elected their own representatives to the Kuk. Today, even though recent changes have brought about the establishment of a Regional Council for the New Territories, the Heung Yee Kuk has maintained its political influence and has members in the Legislative Council. It is somewhat ironic that the New Territories were highly politicized until the urban areas caught up. Elections for village representatives have been fought very bitterly; voters have been flown into Hong Kong from Brit-

ain and elsewhere, and pregnant women have claimed voting rights through the paternity of their unborn children!

This polarized system of rural politics on the one hand, and small-town urban elections on the other, would have been very different if the so-called Young Plan, initiated by the home Labour Government, had been put into effect. It would have created an extensive and elaborate network of electorates with a voting system based on universal suffrage.

By the time the administrative problems were ironed out, the will to reform had dissipated and in the early 1950s China seemed poised to take over Hong Kong. The local Chinese establishment did not wish to relinquish its powers and influence to a more democratic system.

However in 1966, the governor, Sir David Trench, sought to introduce a watered-down version of the Young Plan on local government. But the scheme was engulfed by the riots of 1967, as the Cultural Revolution overflowed into the colony and drowned any hope of immediate reform.

The Union Jack with the flag of the People's Republic of China at the Hong Kong Convention Centre (preceding page); the signing of the Sino-British Joint Declaration, 19 December, 1984 (above); Prime Minister Margaret Thatcher visits Beijing to discuss the future of Hong Kong, 1982 (below)

ever, the last series of District Board contests in 1988 saw a fall in voter turnout. The number of votes cast represented just over 30 percent of the 1.4 million registered voters. Disappointment over the slow rate of progress in the democratization of the Legislative Council has led to a decline in participation in these elections. Nev-

Yet the Hong Kong Government was becoming more aware of the abyss between the administration and the people of Hong Kong and in 1968 set up the City District Office scheme. The government, for the first time, was anxious to know the aspirations and fears of the ordinary men and women in the colony.

In recent years the shadow of 1997 has spurred on the government to take further steps to become more responsive to its constituency and to the people by expanding the system of local government. A Green Paper issued in June 1980 entitled 'A Pattern of District Administration in Hong Kong' reviewed earlier steps in consultation and community development, such as the Fight Crime Committees and the Mutual Aid Committees formed in the government housing blocks, and heralded the creation of 19 District Boards. The principle of direct election, with suffrage for all adults over the age of 21 who have lived in the districts for a minimum of seven years, was accepted in time for the first elections of 1982. But as recently as 1985, when there was greater enthusiasm for participation in elections, only just over half of the 426 District Board members were elected by popular vote. The remainder were either appointed or ex officio. As commentators have pointed out, these local elections were regarded by the participants as a run-up to direct elections to the Legislative Council in 1991. How-

ertheless, the District Boards, both in the urban areas and in the New Territories, do have indirect input into the membership of the legislative body.

The District Board members select ten Legislative Councillors through an electoral college. The rationale behind this indirect method of selecting representatives to the law-making body, according to the government Green Paper, is to secure 'a reasonably balanced geographical distribution of the seats'. Despite criticism of the system, this method of constraining grassroots participation in the electoral system to the Legislative Council, locally perceived as Hong Kong's parliament, has been retained.

However, the situation changed after the negotiations with China in 1982-4. Sir Geoffrey Howe, the British foreign secretary at the time of the Joint Declaration, announced in April 1984 that '. . . during the years immediately ahead the government of Hong Kong will be developed on increasingly representative lines'. This has been done through two important innovations.

Firstly, elected members have been introduced to the Legislative Council and their number has progressively increased, albeit through the indirect method of selection by an electoral college and by elections within nine functional constituencies representing the professions and trade union organizations. The Legislative Council consists of 57 members, with the governor as presiding officer. The membership is divided between elected and officially appointed representatives. At present, official and ex officio members outnumber elected representatives. Moreover, when the council is in session, it meets weekly, which is more frequently than in the days before reform.

The second feature of representative government has been the introduction into the Executive Council—Hong Kong's cabinet—of a proportion of members from the lower house, the Legislative Council.

A full parliamentary system for Hong Kong is still far from realization. It is clear that, given the British Government's attitude, especially towards Chinese antipathy to a democratic parliamentary system, with ministers answerable to a house of elected representatives, such a system will not be introduced into Hong Kong to ensure the complete autonomy of the region after 1997. Indeed, it is the Chinese position that the Basic Law will not permit such drastic changes. The Basic Law was approved by the National People's Congress on 4 April 1990 which, under the terms of the Joint Declaration, provides the constitutional authority for the future administrative region. Hong Kong Government policy is set out in its White Paper (10 February 1988), 'The Development of Representative Government: the Way Forward'. Its cautious guidelines indicate no bold measures for the immediate future: first, evolution is to suit Hong Kong conditions; second, development should be prudent and gradual; finally, the system to be in place by 1997 should permit a smooth transition between the two governments and a high degree of continuity thereafter. In March 1990, the White Paper was superseded by an announcement increasing the number of directly-elected and functional constituency seats in 1991. This came in response to calls for greater democracy in the light of the June 1989 massacre in Beijing.

Democracy in Hong Kong has always been a frail plant as a result of colonial over-

protection, which grew out of the assumption that the Hong Kong people were not ready to determine their own future. The course of events dictated by Britain in the last decade has only confirmed the policy of extreme conservatism. Hong Kong, in retrospect, can be seen as a fatally flawed creation of Western commerce. It has been, since its beginnings, an anomaly, especially in its own administrative and economic efficiency vis-à-vis China; its very success has only served to make any political aspirations towards democracy all the more unrealistic.

Growing demands for directly-elected seats in the Legislative Council (preceding page); the original statue of the 'Goddess of Democracy' was erected in Tiananmen Square during the 1989 protest. This was pulled down, but a replica was raised in Victoria Park, Hong Kong, soon afterwards (above)

The Black Sun

The Shadow of Tiananmen Over Hong Kong

A black sun has appeared in the sky of my motherland and republic.

(Wu'er Kaixi, student leader in Beijing, 15 June 1989)

The movement for reform in China erupted into two months of mass demonstrations throughout the Mainland from April to June 1989; it set off a glow of sympathy and hope in Hong Kong as over a million local residents marched through the streets of the colony demonstrating their support for the Beijing students. In the weeks before the massacre at Tiananmen Square, the mood in Hong Kong was one of innocent optimism, as if the demonstrators in the territory were saying to their brothers and sisters north of the border, 'We want you to share the freedom which we enjoy in Hong Kong'.

It was of course a naive hope, and as news of the events of 4 June 1989 reached the territory, it set off an explosion of impotent rage and frustration, and also of profound grief. A day of mourning was announced; commercial activities were suspended. People carrying wreaths draped with black and white ribbons of crepe, Western and Chinese symbols of death, formed an angry barricade outside the offices of the New China (Xinhua) News Agency, the putative head-quarters of the People's Republic in Hong Kong.

The sun was indeed black, even in Hong Kong. The link between politics and economics was demonstrated in no uncertain way as the bottom dropped out of China trade for several months after the Tiananmen affair. Contracts with Mainland ventures were cancelled, joint ventures were stalled; a year passed before business began to pick up. Chinese trade had been the major driving force for Hong Kong's economic growth, but this major set-back appeared to be ushering in a period of near stagnation: very low rates of growth as compared with the double digit milestones of the previous decade.

The political outlook is still equally grim and the implications of the Tiananmen affair can only be seen as a defeat for the Alliance Movement and for all those who fought for democracy in Hong Kong and China. The final drafting of the Hong Kong Basic Law in Guangzhou in February 1990 was accomplished without fully consulting the Hong Kong people, as promised in both the Chinese and

English versions of the Joint Declaration. This was achieved through a secret deal between the British Government in London and the Mainland Government in Beijing. But the Chinese Government have threatened potential difficulties for the holders of British Dependent Territories and British National Overseas passports. They have strenuously objected to British proposals to grant 50,000 Hong Kong heads of households British passports conferring the right of abode in Britain. In doing so, they have browbeaten the Thatcher government into accepting the principle that the great majority of Hong Kong people will be citizens of the People's Republic of China.

China had repeatedly insisted that it would not countenance any decisive steps towards representative government in Hong Kong through the introduction of directly elected members to the colony's Legislative Council. However, it did agree to a programme of reform, outlined in the section on constitutional changes in Hong Kong. The damage is already done, however, as there is now no hope for a democratically elected majority of executive members in the Legislative Council as a bulwark against possible future Chinese incursions during the remaining years of British rule.

In accepting these Chinese remarks on constitutional development in Hong Kong, Douglas Hurd, ex-Prime Minister Thatcher's third foreign secretary after Sir Geoffrey Howe, apparently settled for what was described for public consumption as 'the best prize'. Hurd has feebly attempted to fob off critics in Britain and Hong Kong with the vainglorious notion that China may be persuaded to better the deal in 1995.

Moreover, the Basic Law promulgated in China in April 1990 will allow for suppression of any activity in Hong Kong deemed to threaten public security and unity in China, including criticism of prevailing conditions across the border. The threat to the continuance in Hong Kong of the present system of government, already far from being representative, is grave indeed.

This then is Hong Kong's black sun: the eclipse may be a long one. For worse, not for better or worse, Hong Kong is now bound by history and Chinese law to the fate of that tumultuous country.

The end has come for 'The Colony that Never Was'.

Sorrow and indignation against the events in Beijing expressed by Hong Kong citizens in Chater Gardens, Central, June 1989

THE INTERNATIONAL CITY

No other place in the world makes of itself so perfect a spectacle: extravagant, electric, mesmeric in its beauty, equal to any biblical view the Devil might have shown Christ from the mountain-top as an advertisement for the superiority of worldly goods.

The famous view from the Peak reflects a journalist's ecstatic comments to some extent. Amid the thickets of glittering office towers, which proliferate in Central and Wan Chai, the two banking towers—the Hongkong and Shanghai Bank and its ideological adversary, the Bank of China—stand out in that crowded scene of buildings as temples to Mammon.

The elegant Hongkong and Shanghai Bank

building, designed by the British architect Sir Norman Foster, is proportioned like a modern cathedral and represents a perfect fusion of technology and function.

By contrast, the twin-masted bamboo-shoot tower, by I M Pei, dominates the view not only because of its great height—it is at present Hong Kong's tallest building—but because of its political significance.

But the landscape of Hong Kong is not all high-rise. The famous view from the Peak is framed by craggy mountains that

make up so much of the territory, and by the intervening waters.

The densely populated stretches of Tsim Sha Tsui and the adjoining suburbs are visible from our lookout on the Peak. A different panorama lies beyond the frenetic fringe of activity in Kowloon. Once past the mountain barrier of Lion Rock, Kowloon Peak and Tai Mo Shan, we can discover some ten satellite towns, all of which have sprung into existence in the past 20 years, each nominally self-contained with the capacity to accommodate about 500,000 people.

A growing proportion of Hong Kong's six million inhabitants live and work in, or commute to Hong Kong and Kowloon from these satellite towns. This is the result of a far-reaching plan to accommodate the overflow from Kowloon and to develop the rural districts, integrating them into the economy of South China.

One of the themes of this book is the revolutionary way in which over the past 40 years Hong Kong has become an integrated city-state without political independence. That integration has come about by the construction of superhighways, tunnels, an underground

railway system linking Hong Kong with Kowloon and the New Territories, and the electrified Kowloon–Canton Railway. The immediate result of this remarkable transport system has been to knit together the rural and urban population into a feverishly busy economy.

Jan Morris, who has described Hong Kong many times, sums up these recent developments memorably in her recent preface to the book Building Hong Kong:

This outward and upward movement— for Hong Kong everywhere is a vertical concentrated city like Manhattan—is the result of 'two great historical progressions': the industrialization of Hong Kong and the liberalization of the post-war British Empire. Today we see Hong Kong transformed from a colonial outpost on the China coast into a truly modern international metropolis.

The new headquarters of the Hongkong and Shanghai Bank, Central, was designed by architect Sir Norman Foster, and built at a cost of HK$5.3 billion (preceding page); the Bank of China Tower, designed by Chinese-American architect I M Pei, is presently the tallest building in the world outside New York and Chicago (left)

BIBLIOGRAPHY

Balke, Gerd (ed.) *Hong Kong Voices*. Longman, Hong Kong, 1989.

Berry Hill Galleries Inc. *Merchants, Mandarins and Mariners: Nineteenth Century Paintings of the China Trade*. New York, 1979.

Birch, A and Cole, M *Captive Christmas*. Heinemann Asia, Hong Kong, 1979.

Birch, A and Cole, M *Captive Years*. Heinemann Asia, Hong Kong, 1982

Bonavia, D *Hong Kong 1997: The Final Settlement*. South China Morning Post Publications, Hong Kong, 1983.

Briggs, A *Victorian Cities*. Penguin, London, 1982.

Cameron, N. *An Illustrated History of Hong Kong*. Oxford University Press, Hong Kong, 1991.

Cameron, N. *Hong Kong: The Cultured Pearl*. Oxford University Press, Hong Kong, 1978.

Christman, Margaret C S *Adventurous Pursuits: The Americans and the China Trade 1784-1844*. Published for the National Portrait Gallery by the Smithsonian Institute Press, Washington DC, 1984.

Coates, A *A City of Light*. Macmillan, Hong Kong, 1982.

Coates, A *Myself A Mandarin*. Fredrick Muller, 1968; Heinemann (Asia) 1975.

Coates, A *Whampoa*. South China Morning Post, Hong Kong, 1980.

Coates, A *The Road*. HarperCollins, 1949.

Collis, M *Foreign Mud*. Faber, London, 1946.

Eitel, E J *Europe in China*. Oxford University Press, Hong Kong, 1983 reprint of the original 1895 edition.

Endacott, G B *A History of Hong Kong*. Oxford University Press, Hong Kong, 1973.

Endacott, G B *Hong Kong Eclipse*. (with additional material by A Birch) Oxford University Press, Hong Kong, 1978.

England, J and Rear, J *Industrial Relations and Law in Hong Kong*. Oxford University Press, Hong Kong, 1981.

Faure, D, Hayes, J, and Birch, A (eds.) *From Village to City*. University of Hong Kong, Centre of Asian Studies, Hong Kong, 1984

Harris, P *Hong Kong: A Study in Bureaucratic Politics.*
    Heinemann Asia, Hong Kong, 1978.

Hong Kong Government, Museum of Art *The Pearl River in the*
    Nineteenth Century. Hong Kong, 1981.

Hong Kong Government, Museum of History *History Around Us.*
    Hong Kong, 1982.

Hong Kong Government, Information Department 1985 *Yearbooks.*
    Hong Kong, 1985 and subsequent years.

Horstman, C *The China Coast: Ships, Ports and People.*
    Hong Kong, 1980.

Hughes, R *Borrowed Place, Borrowed Time.* Andre Deutsch,
    London, 1968.

Miners, N *The Government and Politics of Hong Kong.* 4th edition,
    Oxford University Press, Hong Kong, 1986.

Miners, N *Hong Kong Under Imperial Rule 1912-1941.*
    Oxford University Press, Hong Kong, 1987.

Miners, N *The Government and Administration of Hong Kong.*
    3rd edition. Oxford University Press, Hong Kong, 1981.

Morris, J *Among the Cities.* Oxford University Press, New York, 1985.

Morris, J *Hong Kong: Xianggang.* Viking, London and New York, 1989.

Building Hong Kong, with an essay by Jan Morris.
    Formasia, Hong Kong, 1989.

Newall Beaumont *The History of Photography.*
    Museum of Modern Art, New York, 1982.

Pope-Hennessy, J *Half Crown Colony.* London, 1969.

Rafferty, Kevin *City on the Rocks: Hong Kong's Future.*
    Viking, London, 1989.

Sayer, G R *Hong Kong: Its Birth, Adolescence and Coming of Age.*
    Hong Kong University Press, Hong Kong, 1937.

Turner, J E *Kwang Tung or Five Years in South China.*
    Hong Kong, Oxford Universtiy Press, reprint, 1982.

Waley, A *The Opium War Through Chinese Eyes.* Allen and Unwin,
    London, 1958.

FOOTNOTES

1   The British imperial outposts in the Far East and Southeast Asia were all
     offshore islands of the Eastern Archipelago—Penang, Singapore, Palembang,
     and Labuan.

2   Sayer, G R, *Hong Kong; Its Birth, Adolescence and Coming of Age,*
     Oxford, 1937, page 190.

3   Perhaps the pessimism expressed in an article published in *The Gentleman's
     Gazette,* a Bombay magazine, around 1845 was understandable: 'The trade
     in Hong Kong is nought. Ships touch there, but they refuse to break bulk ...
     few would be tempted to dwell, or risk themselves or their goods, where
     none but thieves and vagabonds of all sorts will ever resort ...'

4   Gutslaff had, in the 1830s, worked as an interpreter for Jardine, Matheson and
     Company. As the historian of the firm writes: 'Gutslaff ... pouring a torrent of
     tracts over one side of the *Sylph,* as the drug went over the other, never
     mentions opium by name in his letters.' In 1844 he formed the Chinese
     Christian Union at Hong Kong 'to begin his grand scheme of converting
     China'. Just previously he had, on the death of J R Morrison, the famous
     missionary, been appointed to the post of chief secretary to the superintend-
     ent of trade, a responsible and well-paid post.

5   Hong Kong officially became a colony by the issue of Letters Patent in 1843.

6   Dr Eitel was a member of the Basel Mission, a historian of Hong Kong and a
     government official. He was born in Germany in 1838, arrived in Hong Kong
     in 1862 and retired in Australia in 1897.

7   During the negotiations leading up to the 1898 Convention of Peking, Sir
     Robert Hart, as spokesman for the Chinese Imperial Maritime Customs,
     bargained, in fact, for official recognition of the establishment of the Kowloon
     Commissioner of Customs in Hong Kong, itself to collect duties due to China.
     Eventually, in 1929, this was agreed, however, Chinese representatives of
     Chinese artisans, made in the 1880s and later right up to the 1970s, were
     strenuously opposed.

8   Two years later, in an even more radical outburst, the city was declared to be
     a soviet. On both occasions, these risings of provincial independence,
     coupled with communism, were mercilessly suppressed by Kuomintang
     troops.

9   Major General CM Maltby, the General Officer Commanding, in his dispatch
     on the course of the battle for Hong Kong, put the British casualties at 2,113
     missing and 2,300 wounded. In addition, the other forces incurred casualties.
     Japanese losses were admitted as 2,754. The British claimed a total of 3,000
     Japanese killed and 9,000 wounded. The total invading force was probably
     only 13,000.

10   In 1951 one of these fires led to an incident involving China. In an effort to
     prevent exploitation of these unfortunates for political purposes, the Hong
     Kong Government turned back a delegation from Guangzhou bringing relief
     to the fire victims. A riot at Mong Kok ensued.

11   The trauma following the protracted negotiations in Beijing for Hong Kong's
     political future resulted in three successive years (1982-5) when expenditure
     significantly exceeded revenue. The long-term trend of budget surpluses
     resumed in 1986.

12.   Perhaps this was why the New Territories leaders, through their representative body, the Heung Yee Kuk, came to have much more say in the policies affecting their land and way of life than their urban brothers.

13.   Now a third University of Science and Technology in Sai Kung is well underway.

14.   In a bitter twist of history, the right of abode issue has become, in the late 1980s and in the 1990s, the only remaining area where Hong Kong still relies on Britain to play its imperial role of assuming moral responsibility for its former British citizens. Following persistent lobbying by senior foreign members of the Legislative Council, Baronness Lydia Dunn, Mr Allen Lee, and even the governor himself, the Home Government announced a scheme to confer full British passport rights on some 50,000 households (approximately 225,000 people), including the right to immigrate to the United Kingdom. The rationale is that this insurance policy for the elite of Hong Kong's administra tive, business and professional communities will induce them to stay in Hong Kong. It is hoped that this measure will reassure a small sector of the Hong Kong population by introducing 'token stability' and reassure China that prior to the takeover Hong Kong is not being run down by the loss of key person nel. China has not recognized the necessity of this legislation and has threatened that it will not recognize British passports obtained as part of this scheme. The Immigration Act (July 1990) has received Royal Assent.

15.   Gerd Balke (ed.), *Hong Kong Voices,* Longman, Hong Kong, 1989. It should be noted that the interviews were conducted before the Tiananmen Square massacre, and thus opinions expressed may well have changed.

INDEX

MIS/23/01